Oracles Of Hathor

Magnus Malleus

Malleus Net

Introduction

Alchemy is a spiritual practice that uses material objects to achieve a purifying transformation of the operator's personality, spirit or soul, otherwise known as, "making gold". It was first developed in the remote past in conjunction with the secretive craft arts of dye making and metallurgy. Most books written on Alchemy describe the arcane processes, the *input* of the alchemical transformation. This book is a product of the *output* of that transformation. What you will find in this book is not about the various stages of the occult reaction that result in the creation of gold but reveals the actual gold itself.

My alchemical practice is non-traditional but grouped amongst those appearing throughout history as "Kemetic" Alchemy. Originating in Ancient Egypt, this practice sometimes focuses on Copper as its essential substance as opposed to gold. That is the case with my own practice. Copper is the metal of transmission. Just as the electrical power is transmitted through a house by a network of copper wires, the one hundred transformations documented in this book were transmitted by copper, through a piece of stone, into messages from an Egyptian Goddess. Beyond the actual oracles given by the Goddess Hathor, the short texts appearing on the adjacent pages are the result of liminal and meditative trances experienced in contemplation of the Goddess during the time period the Oracles were transmitted.

How to use this book: You can use any method you choose to select an oracle. You can just open the book to any given page or take a hint from a number that you see or pops into your mind. I like to meditate on the Goddess then roll a pair of percentile dice like the type used in adventure gaming. Each is a 10-sided die one being the 10's and the other counting as the ones. The double zero then counts as 100.

The gold created here is the wisdom shared by a being who is timeless, loving and powerful. I am fortunate and blessed to be chosen as her devoted attendant. The greatest gift she has given me is making me her medium of transmission in this particular time and place.

Why was I chosen to be the earthly messenger of the goddess Hathor? I can only guess that I am only one of many who collectively give a human voice to one who's love extends beyond mortal limits.

— Magnus Malleus, December 18, 2025

1

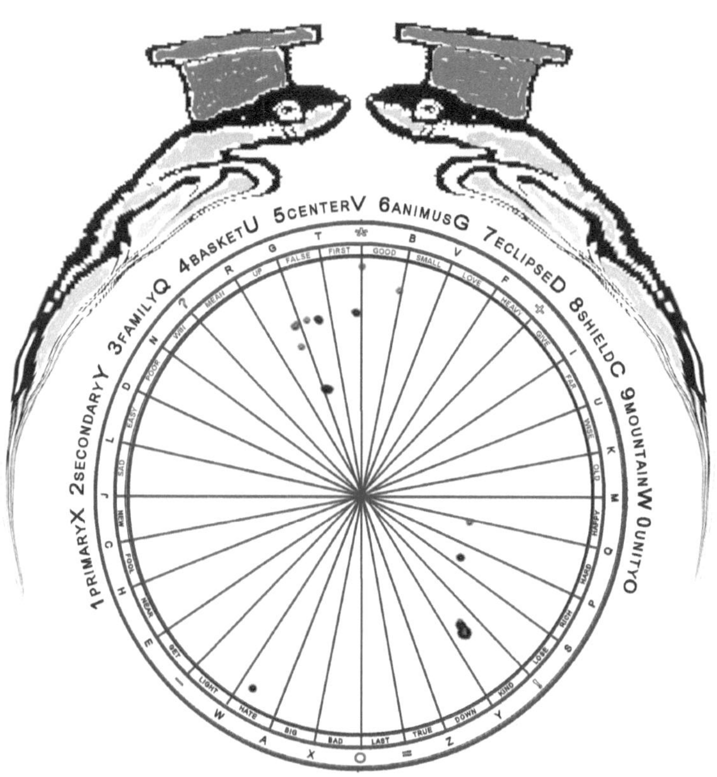

"You are world and species oriented. The aggressive attitude takes pride and pleasure in the family. You pose deceptively with the Body. Physically there is a false pride that hides a shame the Mind wishes to keep a secret."

Saturn is your body. Mercury is your spirit.

It is undignified for a Goddess to descend to time and space- to existence.

She lives in a rarified reality far beyond our grasp.

2

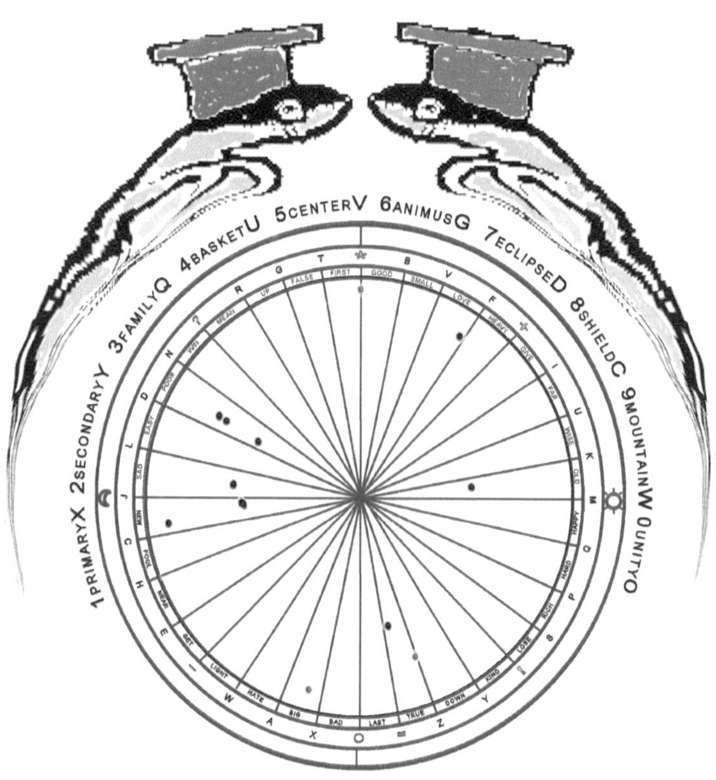

"*You are under a powerful spiritual attack. The Body is targeted but the defense is mounted by cutting off your own spiritual energies and trying to force a change in mental planes. This strategy is not having the desired protective effect and the Body is transforming under the pressure.*"

The wind and the rain carve valleys into you.

To give until it feels like receiving. A worthy goal.

3

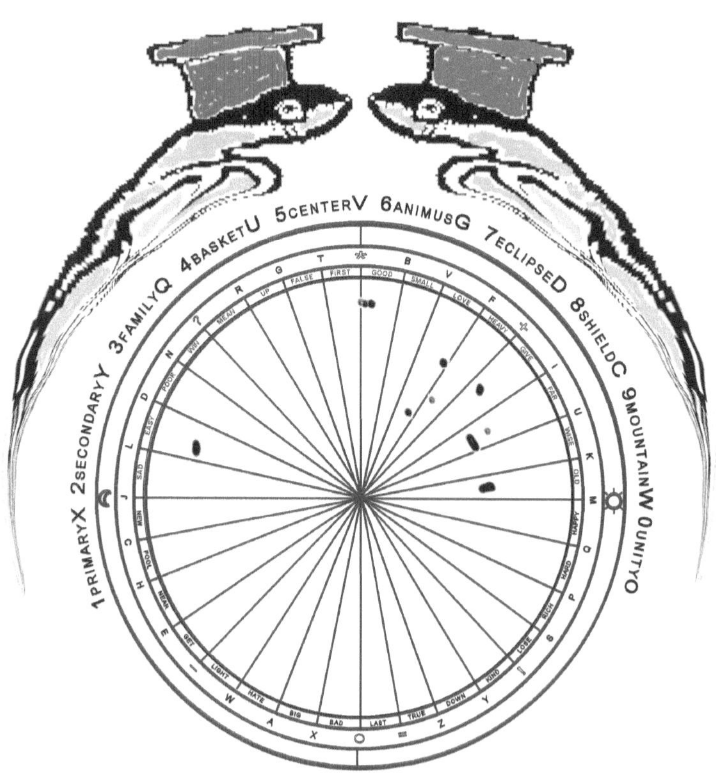

"The Spirit and Body are quiet and unmoving. The Mind is attacking a target using a carefully aimed bolt of Feminine energy. A very old friend or relative some distance away is obstructing your goal. The bolt of Feminine energy will dislodge the obstruction un-noticed by the target. Your meditative state makes the operation easy to perform and requires little recovery."

The divine feminine is the principle of ACTION.

I'm the cup and the sword- the unicorn horn.

4

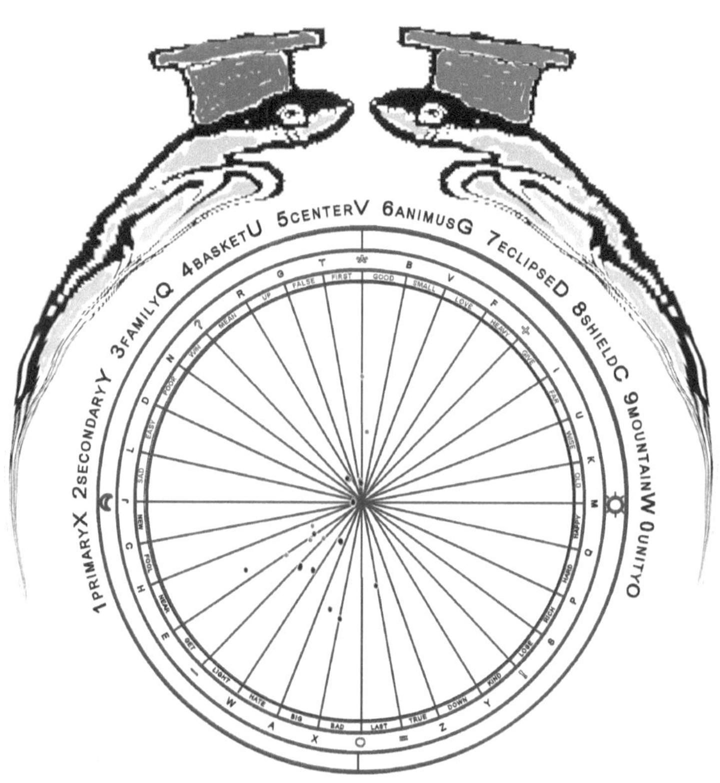

"Spiritual ascension is complete and permanent. The secret of the rising is an incantation. There is an intellectual accompaniment but the formula must not be written down. The intellectual ascension is almost accomplished and the change will be drastic."

The Eyes of Ra are part of you and you belong to them.

Goddesses! I am pure! I am the great white bull!

5

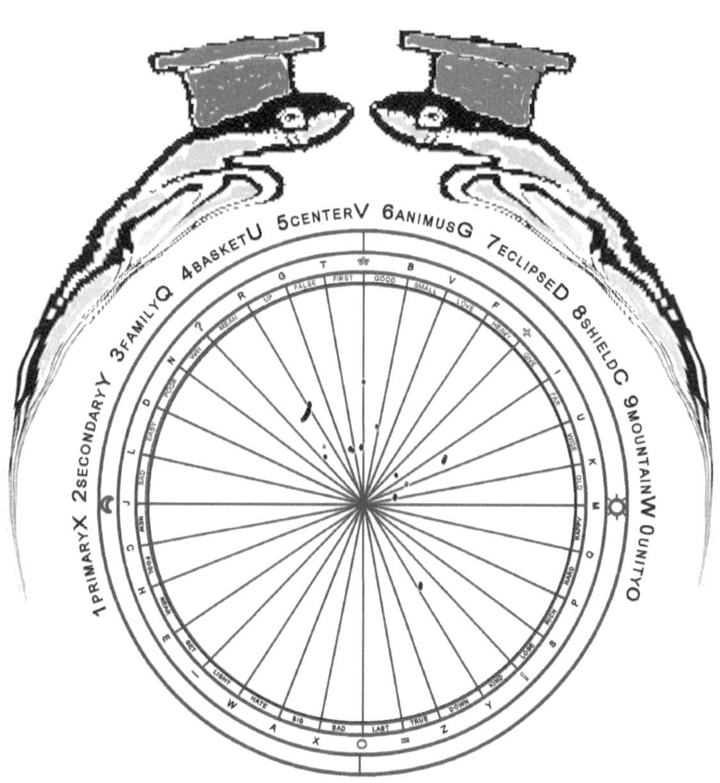

"You are being removed from a position or office. There is a secret plan by the adverse powers to achieve this goal. You are summoning a resistance to the plan but it will be too late to resist."

The best way to learn the science of magic is to learn the science of people.

Embrace and criticize. Criticize and embrace. The real and pure cannot be criticized. The real and pure cannot be embraced.

6

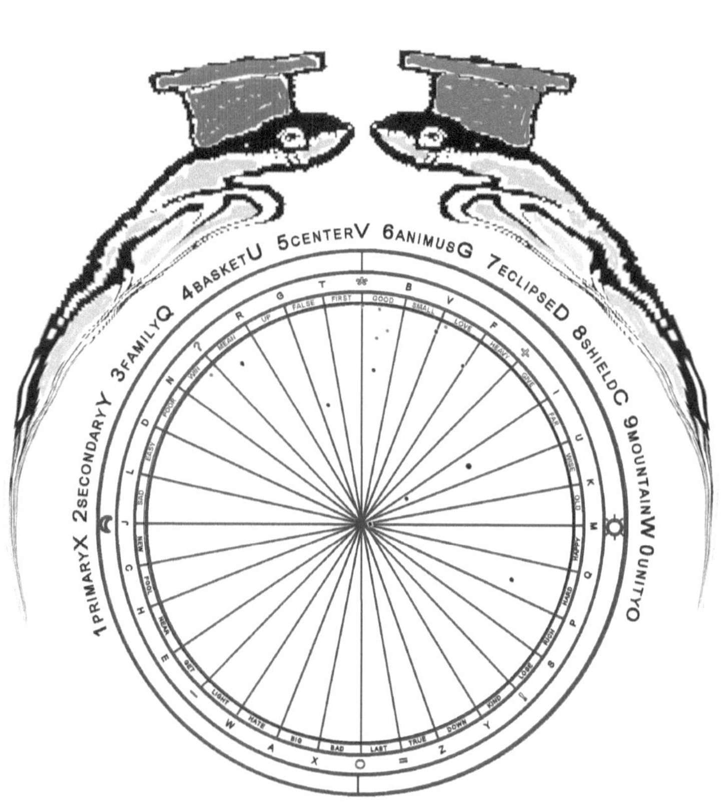

"The Spirit is centered on you and your occult powers. At the same time your Mind and Body are conducting a concentrated attack on a distant adversary. Your Body is in great condition. This ensures your success and your Spirit will triumph through the Body."

There was a time your dreams were in the flesh.

The object of meditation is to make the body stronger. Yes, the body. For that is the source of both mind and spirit.

7

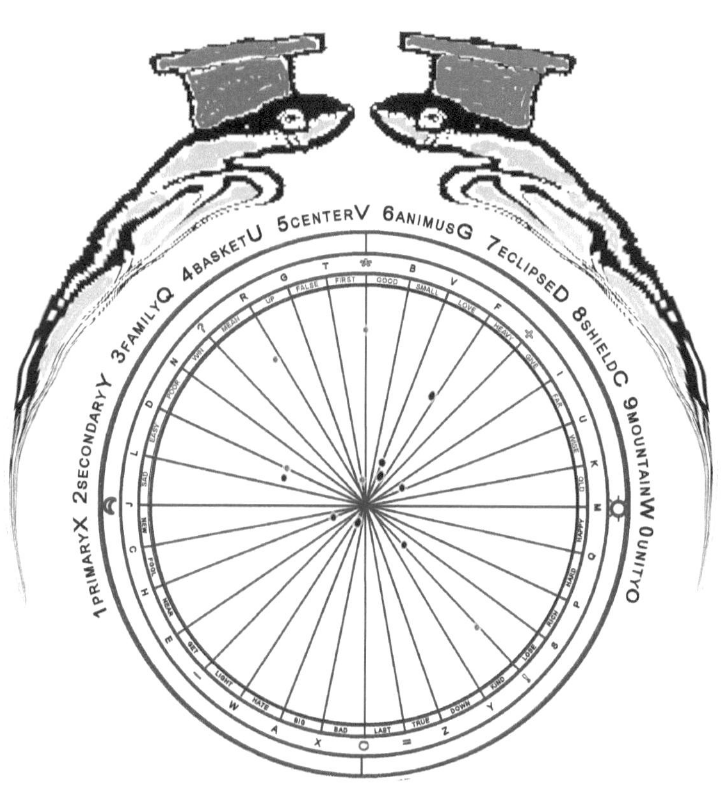

"You have spiritualized the sexual love relation through a powerful Male driving force. The love experienced first mentally and physically are felt as dynamically shifting as the gender energies unite under the influence of the scepter. The Body, and specifically the scepter, is the medium of catalytic reaction."

I am pure, the Temple of the Three Stars is pure.

Split in two. Or three. Die and go to heaven. Then unite and descend back to Earth.

8

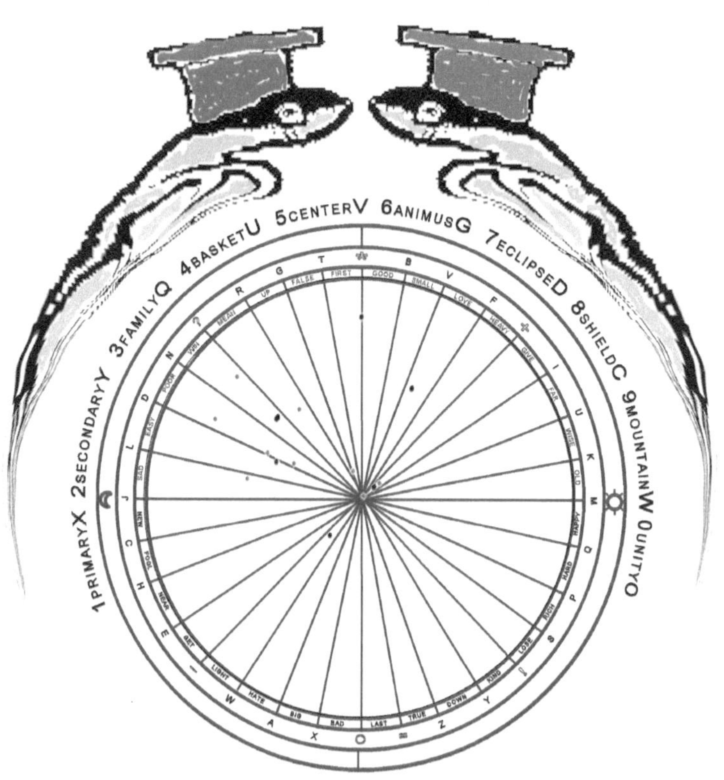

"You are making an intense offering of your Spirit. It is directed to affect a change in the power of the mental plane from the negative to the positive. The result is winning love. It is a drain on your physical state but will ultimately strengthen you."

Divine spirits attend! Hear me! I am MIN! Nephew of Thoth, Son of Isis, King of Memphis, Lord of the Black earth! MIN MENES MINHORUS MINIRTA Kamutef White Bull, Pan, Kamutef of Isis the Sorceress! Bringer of rain! Sower of the seeds of life! Plow of immortal furrows!

Your sulphur is mercurial. Everybody wants some.

9

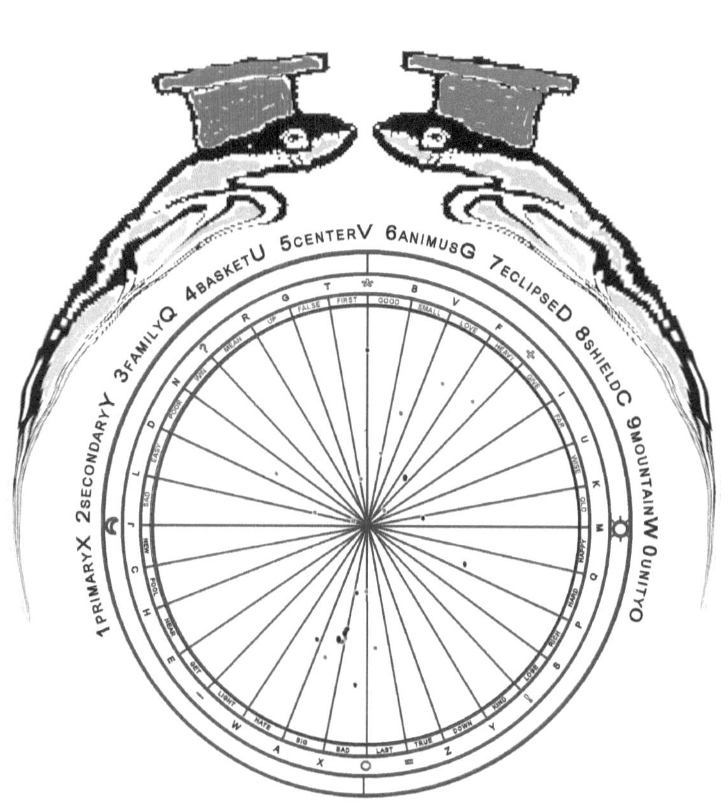

"A conflict or psychic attack has left you severely strained in your mental and physical sexual powers. You were forced to surrender. The damage has shaken your confidence. You must discover a secret to heal."

Hear Me! PRE' KHEPRE KHEPERA APOLYTOS ABSOLUTUS Enabler of the universe, Revealer of the four elements- I offer silent praise to you, the unknowable, the unhearing, unseeing untouching who is beyond time and space who makes possible my divine sacred power.

The new rising sun (Khepr) is used as a symbol of circumradiation (emanation). But we know the sun's rays are the products of transformations, that is, motions. How can the august repose of Ra produce emanations? There is only motion with the birth of the Eyes of Ra goddesses.

10

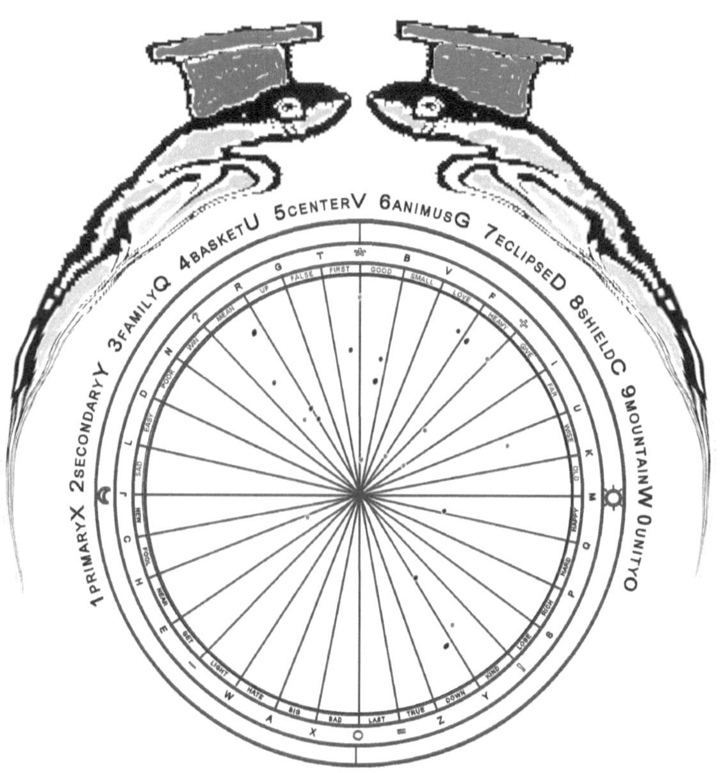

"There is intense physicality and sex drive in you. Your words are positive and powerful tools. You are using them to achieve spiritual balance. This is self oriented activity. The family and those around you are of secondary consideration now. You are an intuitive self creator and your good natured soul tempers your inner strength. Your anger has been sacrificed to strength."

Who transcends life and death and is the four pillars of reality? Author of the sacred geometries which create all souls and symbols. You are the firm Earth of the Sages, stone of the philosophers!

Praise the Eyes of Ra for sending the Horus Eye to heal you. May your lost blood fertilize the barren earth. Soon you will be pure again.

11

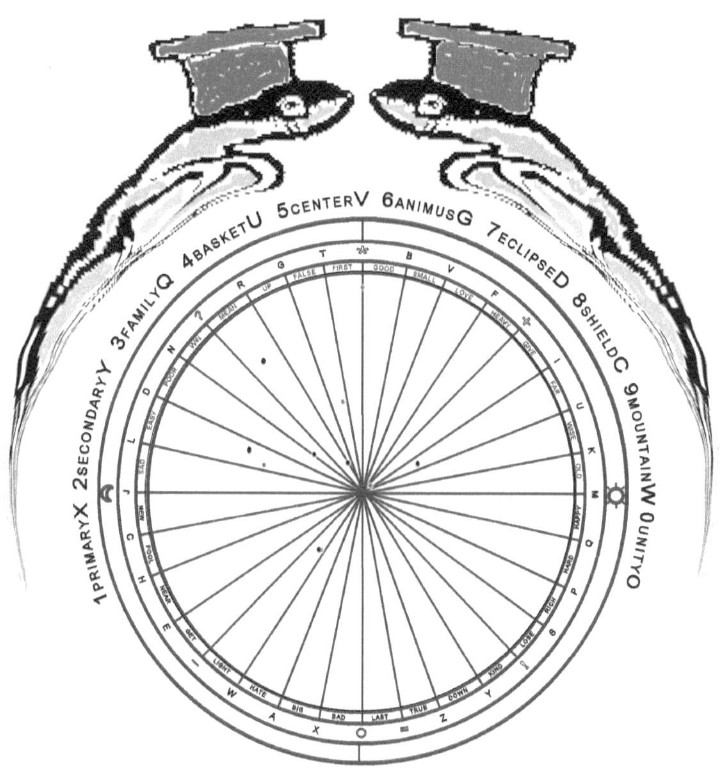

"The Spirit is giving. The gift is conveyed verbally. The Mind and intelligence are constantly growing and changing which can appear as aggression to others. The physical Body is at rest and quiet. Your goals are within reach through a distant vision."

I call on you to deny time and space their dominion so that the Goddesses who are one at one moment may be joined to give me counsel! The Three with many faces, the mothers of the gods, guardians of the pyramids, queens of the sun, join to give me counsel! The Eyes of Ra, ride the golden bark beyond the primal sea through the countless ages and agree to give me counsel!

The reddening begins on the highest plane. But it terminates in your hand.

12

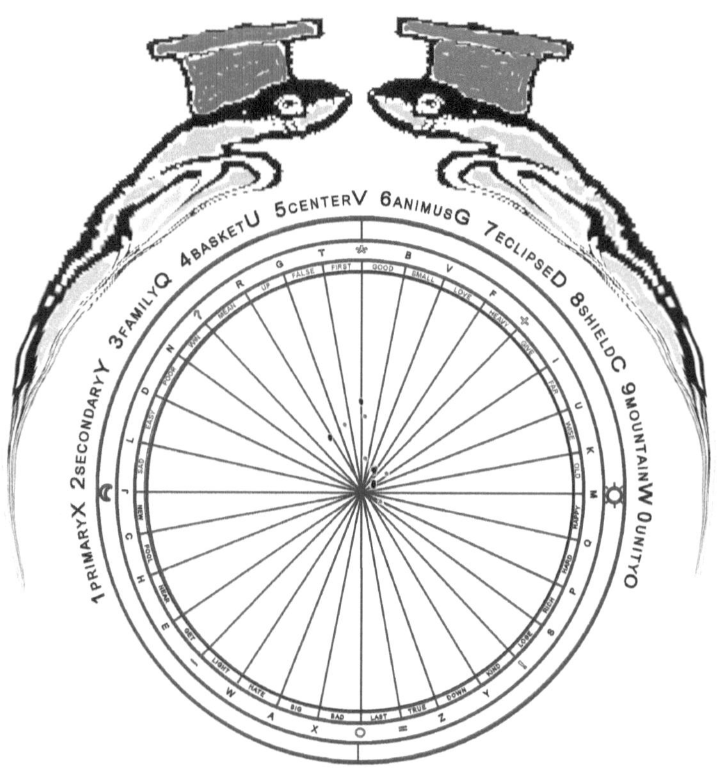

"You are keeping and holding a serious spiritual change or attack. You can use it at your will, for yourself or for others. It is directed by mental force. It is delivered by a pattern of speaking and silence. A dialogue. The message in the dialogue is not necessarily true."

Hear me! I invoke my personal Goddess, divine dark Princess of Kush, she who shares my body and soul. My guide and my mistress who leads me hand in hand through the dense jungles.

Your personal myth is bound up with both past and future. It guides you to new heights and profound depths.

13

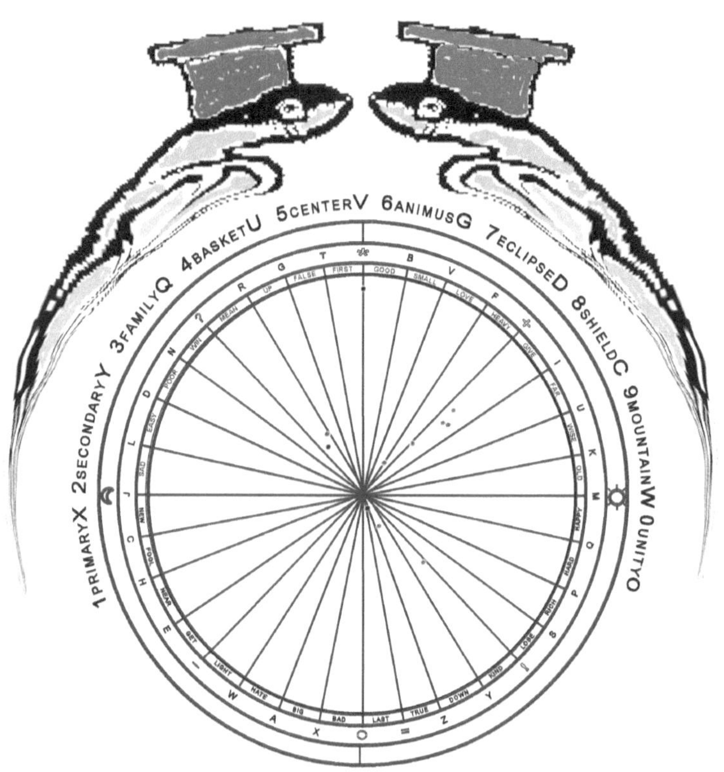

"Your Spirit is in a downward trajectory towards Earth and ocean. The change of planes enables you to deliver an important psychic message to someone who is not ready and doesn't want to receive it. They will be better off for it and their trust is gained."

Powerful Goddess, forever beautiful, daughter of the Black God! Clothe yourself in color! You are the Fire of passion and the Water of life!

When all is done we will be proud of what the sacred light revealed.

14

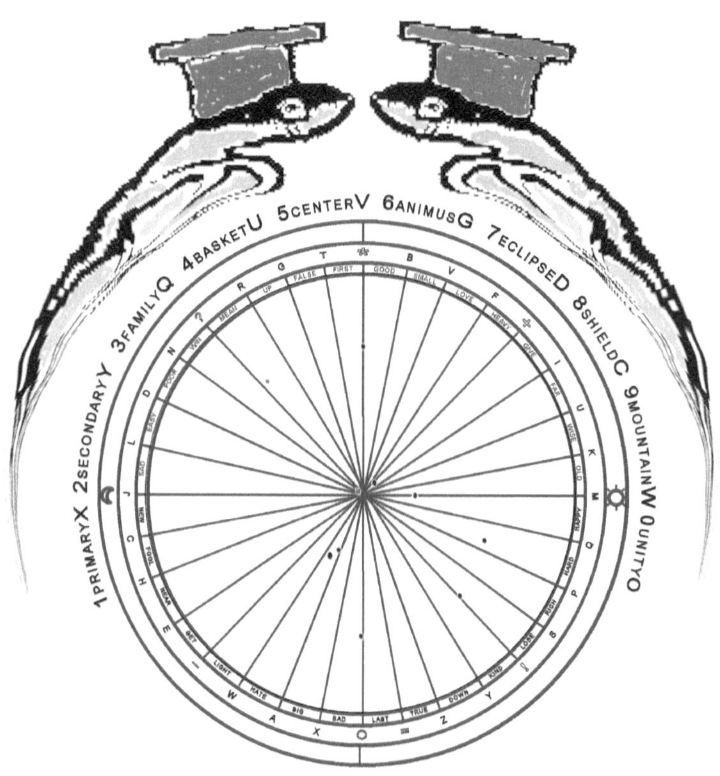

"All of your energies are in balance. You are fortifying your weakened Feminine Spirit with a concentrated mental will to unify it with your strong and aggressive Male consciousness."

Come to me! The white bull calls you! The seer calls you Goddess! In this temple ritual I make this offering of milk and kiss your navel, untamed she-leopard!

Numerical affinity_ 3 to 4:

Alchemical elements Sulpher (Fire, Energy), Earth (Salt, Matter), Mercury (Air, Water, Change).

Alchemists correctly identified air and water as catalysts of chemical change in the combined element Mercury. Air and water are the modes analysis and synthesis. The affinity between three and the reflective four are shown by the Alchemical alternation.

15

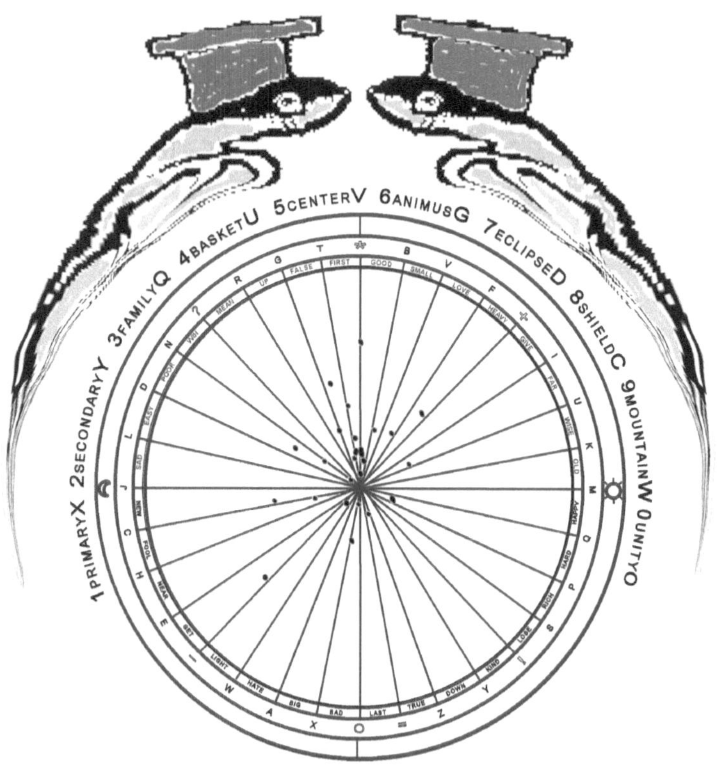

"You are experiencing a spiritual re-orientation from a jarring Mind awakening event. You have reached a difficult conclusion after hard consideration. You are in need of protection and will need to keep it to yourself, and think sharp to handle the problem. But the solution is right before you."

Grant me your sacred charms, hidden secrets and keep my horn strong! Ancient and original Eye of Ra you are-

Heat of the sun, flow of the river

Cut of the blade, bite of the tooth

Scent of the flower, storm of the sky

Dance of the body, word of the mouth

As you are saturated by the divine feminine, you then take on the form of the Moon. That is the gift from the goddesses. Bless the Eyes of Ra.

16

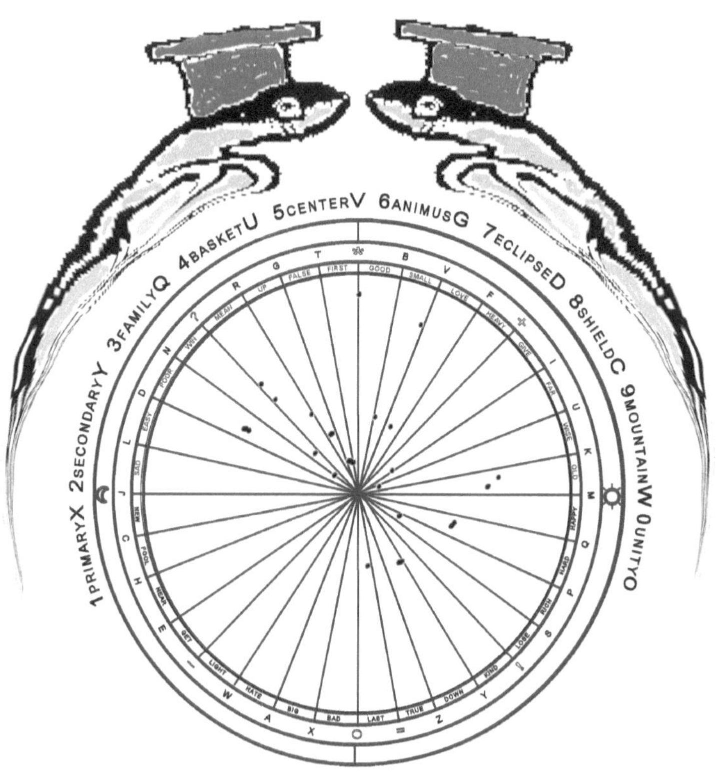

"The integration of the Feminine is complete. What was considered wisdom turned out to be error. Use your Body to focus. Point hands to center. Meditate on the highness of love first and then speak. You must answer a difficult question to form the words you need."

Flight of the wing, swim of the fin

Glint of the gold, weave of the mat

Pitch of the flute, shake of the rattle

Light of the lamp, curve of the bowl

Taste of the honey, veil of the wine

Wax of the seed, wane of the Moon

Course of the star, float of the bark

With my Alchemical vessel I take my place in creation.

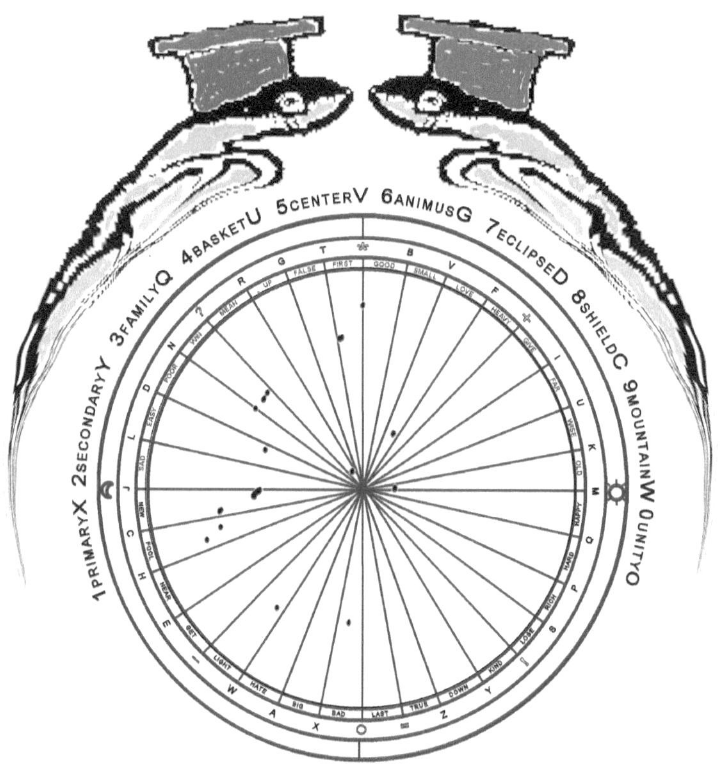

"You have great and fearsome spiritual power. Your Mind serves your Spirit and jumps to conclusions easily because of your willingness to live within your spiritual power. To achieve your goal, you must embrace darkness."

Dream of the sleep, fight of the arm

Shape of the brick, shade of the roof

Beat of the heart, song of the bird

Kiss of the lips, play of the game

Weight of the stone, walk of the leg

Itch of the flea, cool of the fan

Point of the finger, stroke of the hand

The Black Sun, Niger Sol is the entity that absorbs only. It is black, like a black hole absorbing all waves and particles. It is visible / sensible unless enveloped by the same. Then it is invisible. It is Saturn. The body. Prima Materia.

18

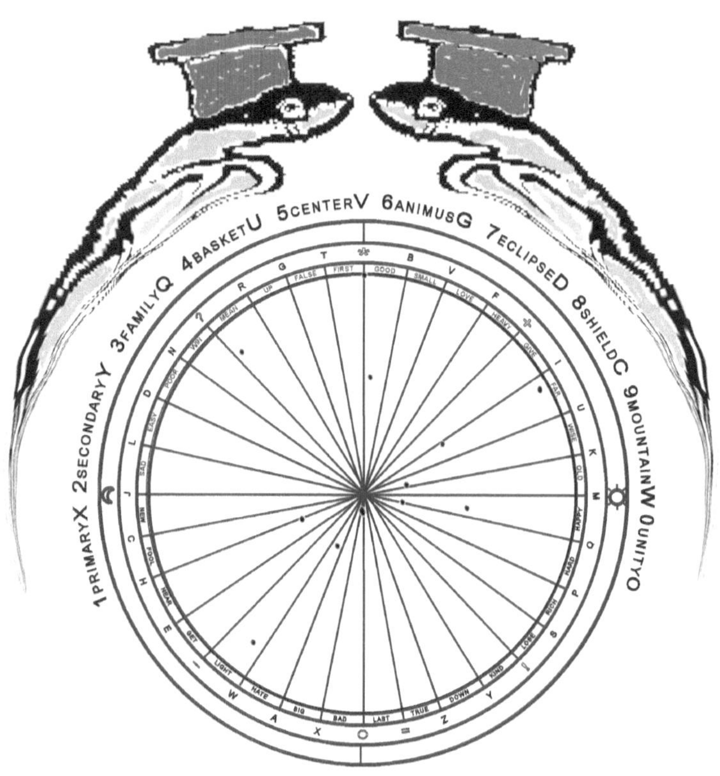

"Independence from the family or group is your focus right now. You are a storm. You reject the feelings of those close to you. It is spiritually painful. You will physically travel away."

Fall of the tree, catch of the snare

Seal of the clay, bend of the reed

Thrust of the spear, opening of the bud

Sting of the scorpion, coil of the serpent

Hear me Goddess! Hear me!

Dedicate yourself to the Goddesses. They may use you as they wish.

19

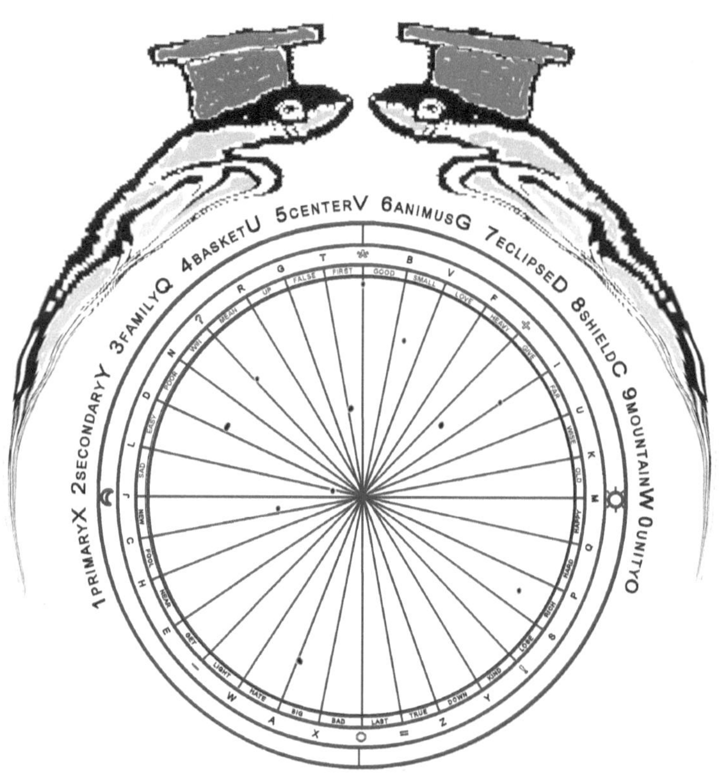

"You are an intensely spiritual person with a strong healthy Body. You need to change your thinking and give up some impulsive tendencies in favor of intuition and analysis."

My seeing stone has penetrated the vessel. Goddess! Pour out your heart to me as I have poured for you. Pour your wisdom into the vessel. Protect my body and subdue my enemies. Hear me Goddess! Hear me!

Like many things, the hardest part of Alchemical transformation is coming down.

20

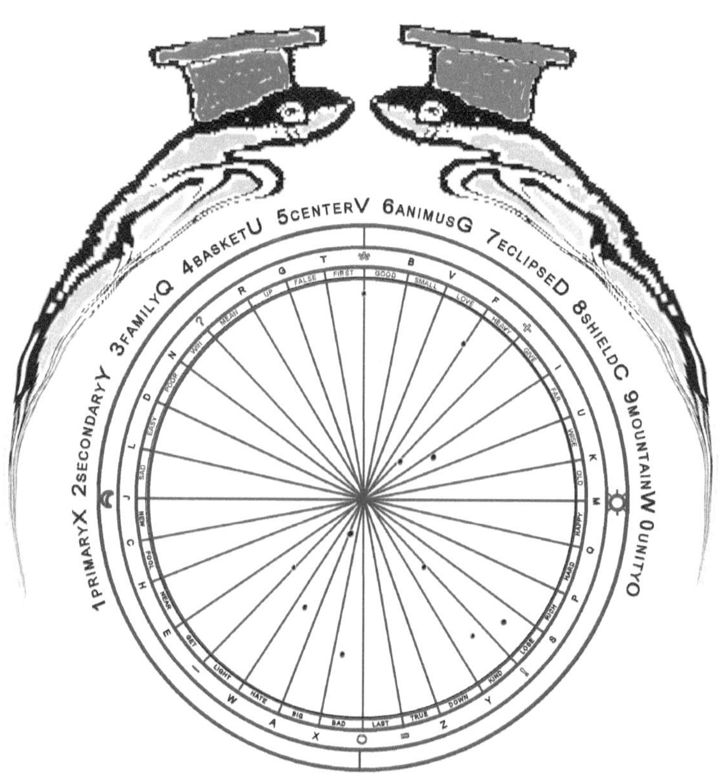

"You are spiritually impulsive and overheated. You are indecisive and it is troublesome. You have had enough talking. Your Body is tense and ready to fight for better or worse."

Hear me! Goddess! You traveled north by the star Polaris to the land of pyramids to become honored as the daughter of RA with names as abundant as your dappled spots- MENHIT, MEKHIT, SHES-METET, PAKHET, ANAT, GETESH, ASTARTE, SEKHMET- You are the Fires of passion and the Waters of life!

The Goddesses are angry. There will be blood on the sand.

21

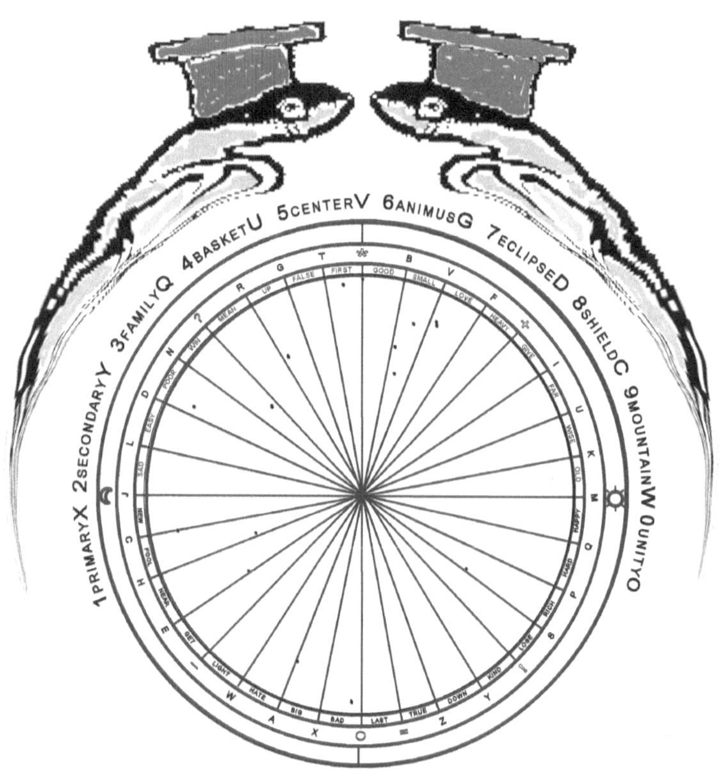

"Your physical Body is in control. Even with the accepting inclination of the Feminine, your Body is overflowing with Male sexual energy. Your Spirit is subservient to the needs and powers of your Body, and your Mind is traveling a path of pleasant but trivial thoughts as if from a book. The Male energy is a protective shield but it doesn't block your intuition."

Hear me! Goddess! By the great flowing Nile you are called by RA, desert bathed, golden, courageous, to guard the Pharaohs in war, destroy their enemies and heal their wounds. Likewise, protect me from angry shadows, demons and ghosts.

Transformation begins with the Moon in the blackness of night, then rises in the glory of pure white Light, only to descend through the forge of Solar rays clothed in fiery crimson.

22

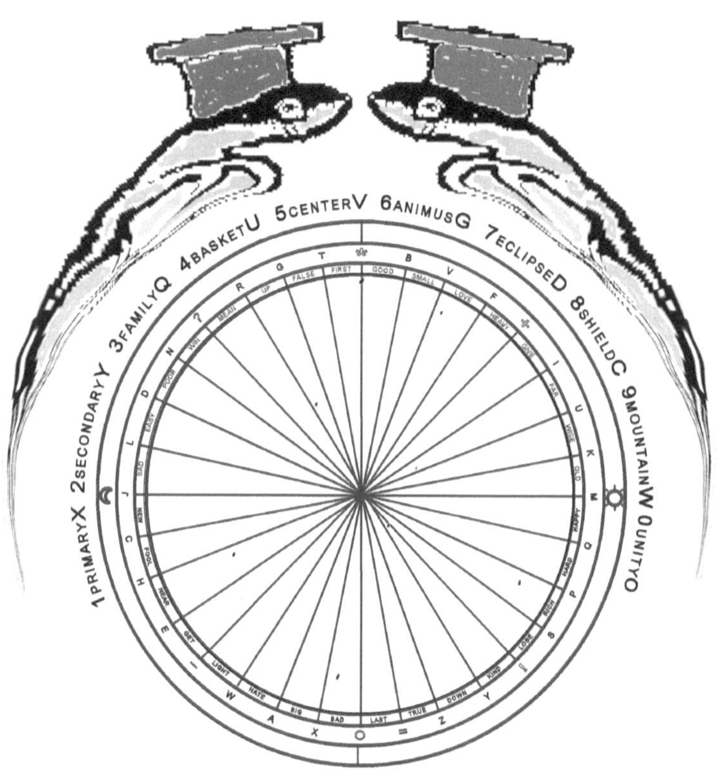

"The Spirit is quiet and at rest. The Spirit is both near and far away having no dimension. The Mind urgently calls to the Sprit to awaken it, tapping into the physical and leaving the Body weak, soft and powerless."

Hear me! Goddess! With fury and cunning, guardians of the realm, you, daughters of RA- MENHIT, MEKHIT, SHESMETET, PAKHET, ANAT, GETESH, ASTARTE, SEKHMET- Let fly the immortal flaming arrows of death!

The Goddesses are part of you. They are ancient and wise. And they never forget. Recline at the feet of Hathor until summoned.

23

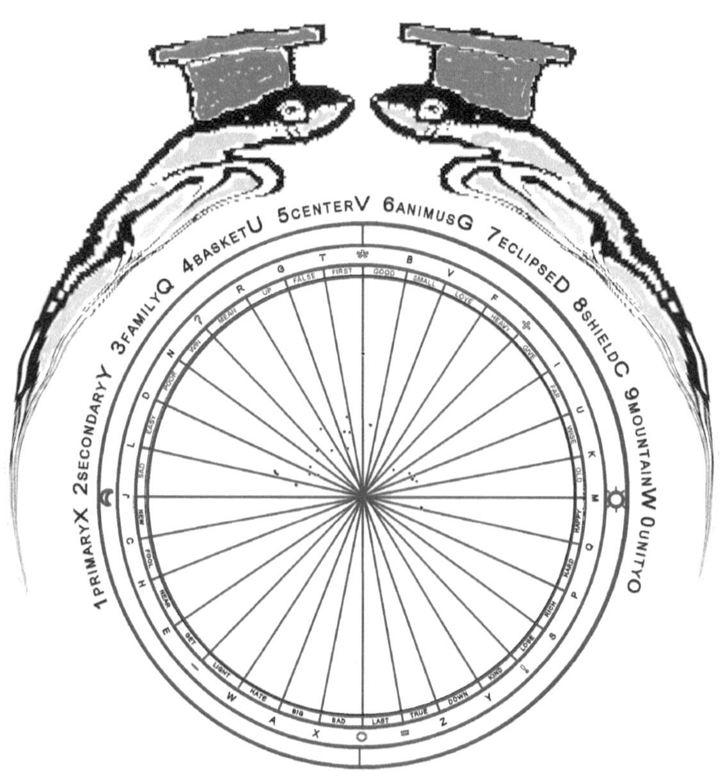

"You are experiencing a gradual and oscillating shift in consciousness from the ego towards the universal whole. You are letting go of the self center that came easily to you in favor of the higher remote. This shift is both intellectual and emotional but not impulsive or logical."

Hear me! Goddess! MENHIT, MEKHIT, SHES-METET, PAKHET, ANAT, GETESH, ASTARTE, SEKHMET Fury of RA, destroyer of the unworthy, subduer of tyrants, spear of kings, driver of the great war chariot- Your renowned bloodlust has cleansed the earth! It is now for you to reap the rewards of noble service and take your place in the starry heavens! With innocent deceit RA soothes your raging heart!

If a Goddess touches you then she exists in you.

24

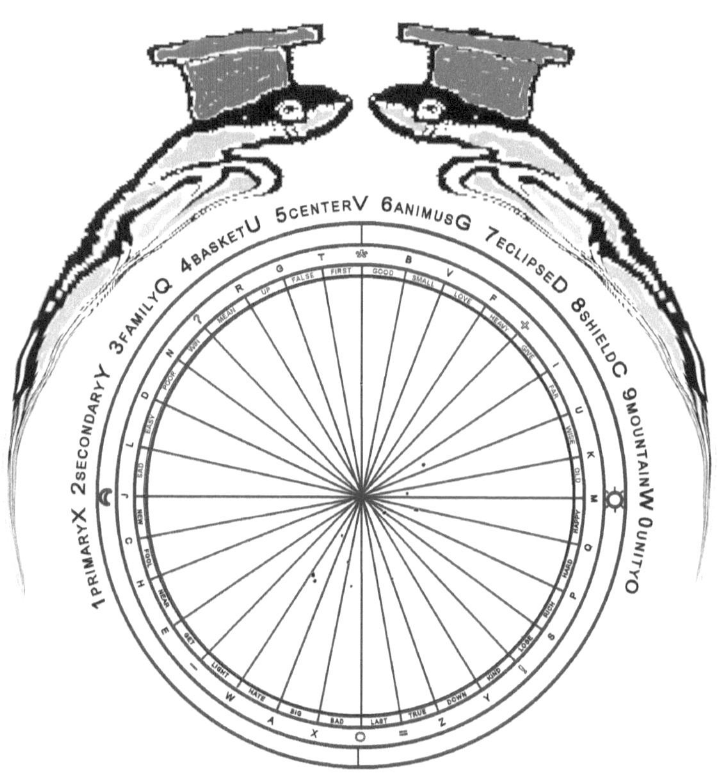

"You are on a path to rebuild love or family connections. Your heart is leading the way past and through painful memories."

Hear me! Goddess! Your task is done. The desert sands are drowned in the blood of the enemy! Disguised with the horns of skyborn love, ascend as the sky goddess HATHOR, mother of gods. Queen of RA, Mother of OSIRIS, Mother of ISIS, Mother of HORUS, Mother of SET.

Your eyes are solar discs when you talk about the things you love.

25

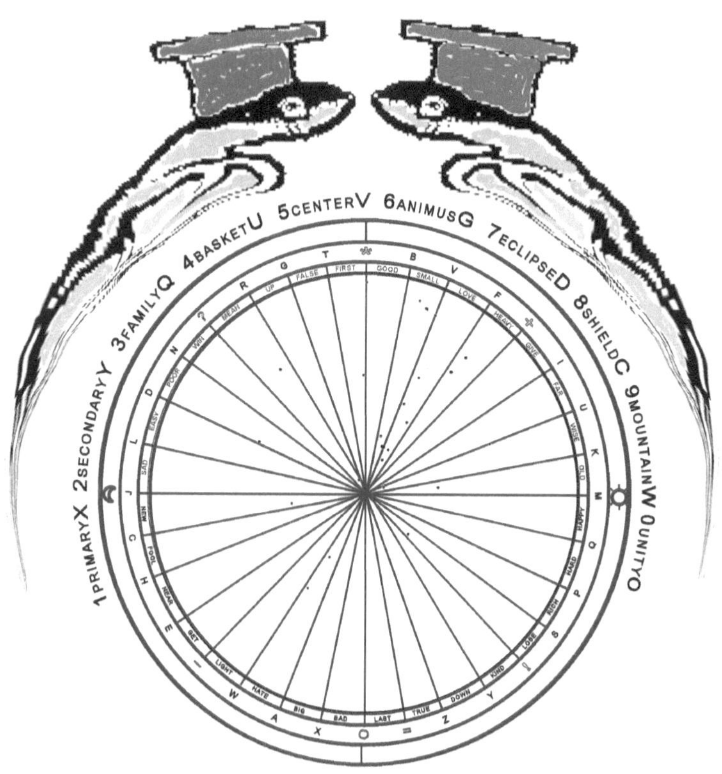

"Your desire for a Woman is eternal. This love is liberating and keeping you centered. You swear an oath to her on a small bone or similar object."

Hear me! Goddess! You HATHOR are the essence of woman. You are cruelty tempered with sweet love! You HATHOR are the Fire of passion and the Water of life! You HATHOR are the golden one- the radiance of RA!

It is fair to judge someone by their idols.

26

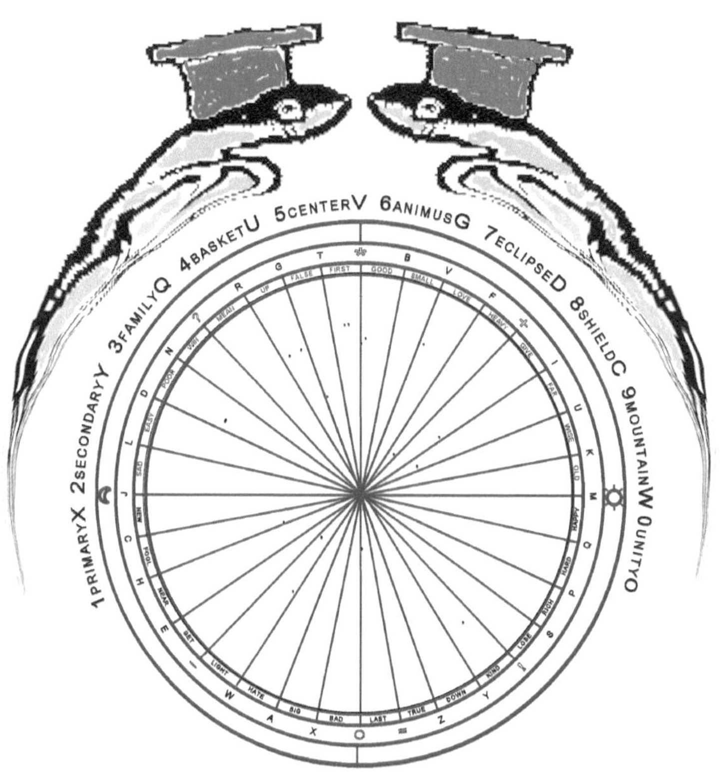

"Your duality, or shadow self is providing a stabilizing and grounding influence on your mental activities. There is a depth and richness to your mental powers resulting from this newly forged bond emanating goodness, love and kindness. Your physical Body is the source and needs to be considered with more respect."

Hear me! Goddess! You HATHOR are proud wife and uraeus, bringer of joy and ecstasy! Your allure is reflected in every mirror! You HATHOR are the divine mistress of love! Mother of all! All shall feast to praise your celestial body and flowing midnight tresses. All shall sing and dance to honor the Eye of Ra!

If you are paper let me write on you. If you are stone let me carve. If you are flesh....

27

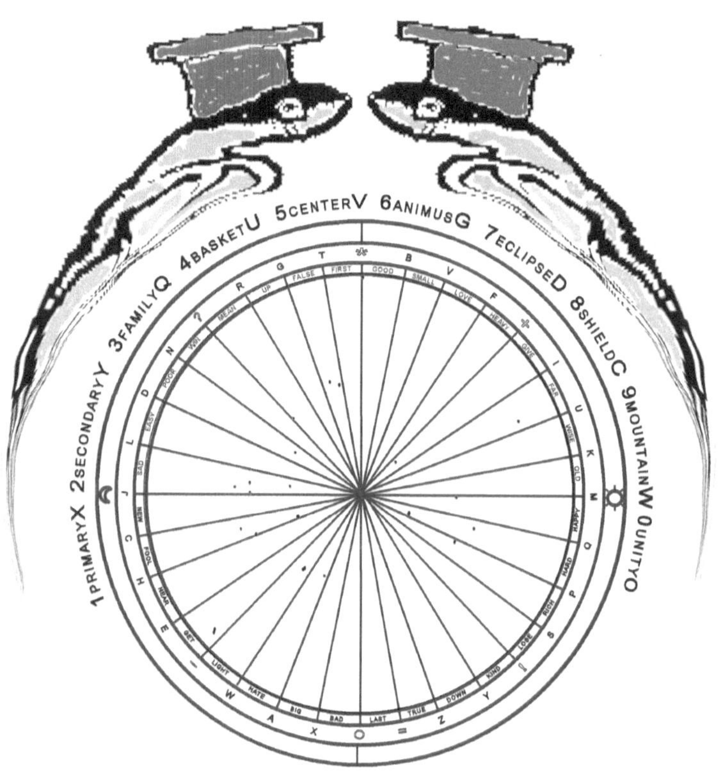

"There is a thought bothering you. You have given yourself over to something. You are not in control. To resolve the problem and regain your power, first submerge the thought in darkness, then suddenly cast illumination on it. As you cast the light on it physically run from it. It will be lost forever."

Hear me! I am MIN! Nephew of THOTH, Son of ISIS, Beloved of the Goddesses! Possessed by the Goddesses! Pursued by the Goddesses! Held fast by the Goddesses! Beloved of the Goddesses! Possessed by the Goddesses! Pursued by the Goddesses! Held fast by the Goddesses! Beloved of the Goddesses! Possessed by the Goddesses! Pursued by the Goddesses! Held fast by the Goddesses! Beloved of the Goddesses! Possessed by the Goddesses! Pursued by the Goddesses! Held fast by the Goddesses!

The transformation of black into white is symbolic death.

28

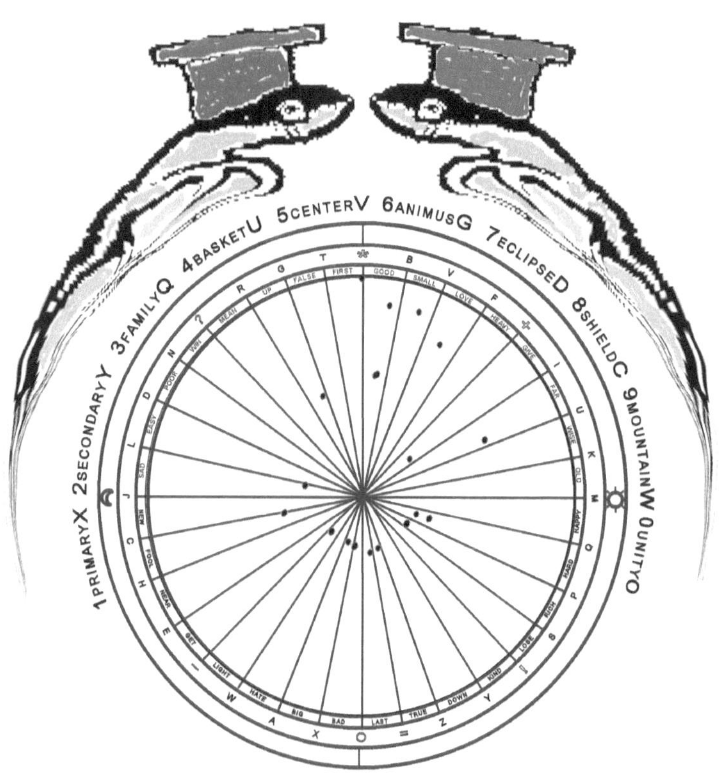

"The focus and power of the Mind are leading the way on a journey transcending the planes of existence. You are seeking a spiritual foundation or historical origin that offers you enhanced protective power to shield others. There is a small but important fertilizing physical and sexual aspect to your journey."

Hear me! I give pleasure to Ma'at! She will favor me! The Goddesses will tell me the truth! I must be satisfied!

I am Min! God of the Black Earth! Consort of the Eyes of Ra! I reach up to the Heavens!

29

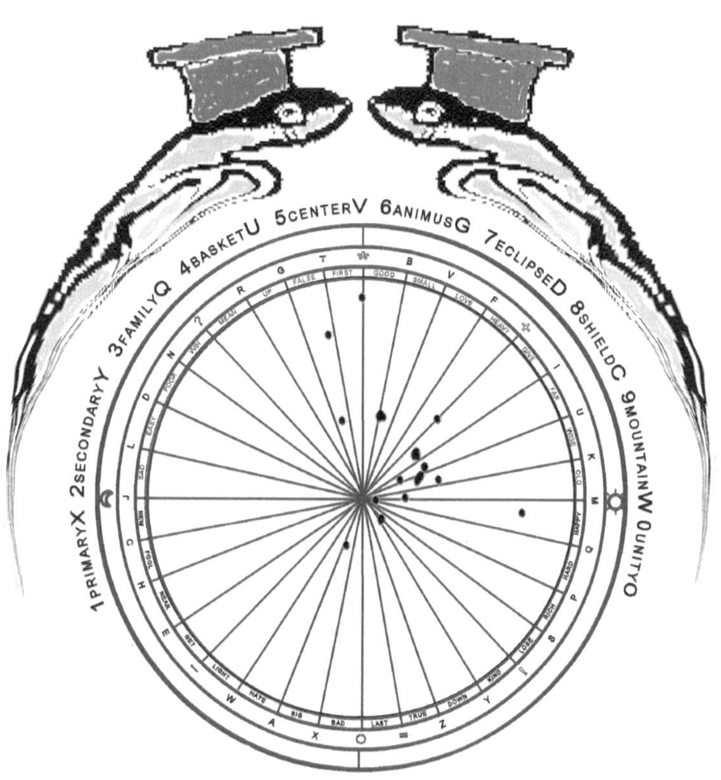

"The Spirit and Mind are in harmony. You must meditate on your love for me. You must consciously take in my love and remain silent about it. Beneath your easy going exterior lies a great depth and power expressed in the Male active and aggressive energies."

Hear me! THOTH THOTHERMIS HERMES change their words into the magical symbols at my disposal so that I can know their hearts. So that I can accept the counsel of the Eyes of RA and be given the powers of their strength, courage and love. Hear me! THOTH THOTHERMIS HER-MES, I, offer you the seeing stone of PRE' KHEPRE KHEPERA APOLYTOS ABSOLUTUS!

Hathor is your Mother.

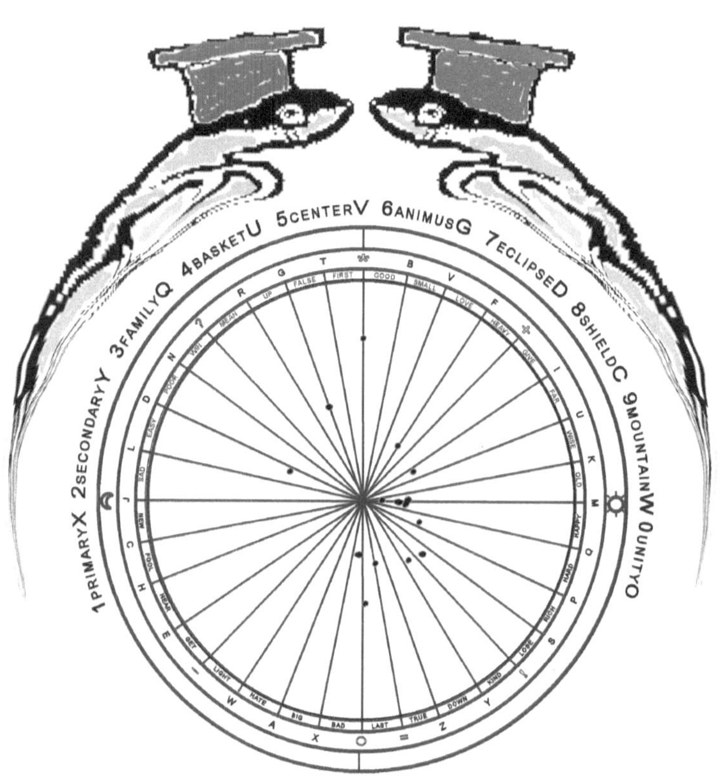

"*You are a master of spiritual energy. The key to your power is to concentrate on the present situation and disregard the remote. To use your power, bond with your opposite gender self. You will defeat an adversary.*"

Hear me! Great god of wisdom and magic engrave the words of the Goddess on the papyrus strip. Great god of wisdom make the symbols appear to my eyes! Speaker of truth, Lover of Ma'at, Weigher of hearts, Master of symbols.

Should men not worship gods nor women the goddesses?

31

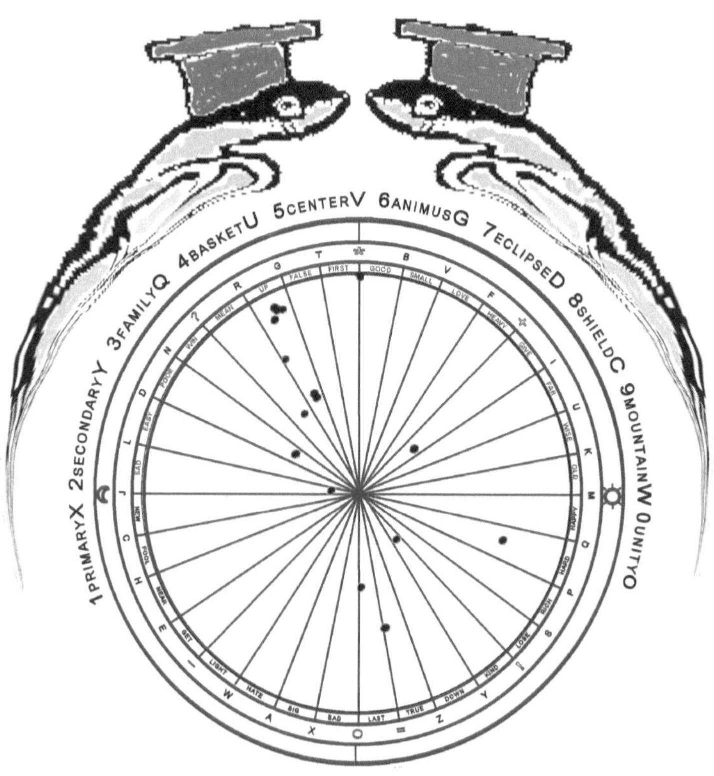

"Your Spirit is heavy with sadness. Your thoughts are humble and filled with sympathy. Your Body can truly fly with the right words."

Hear me! I must be Satisfied! Compel the words from the Eyes of Ra! Compel the divine symbols to descend from the Air of Heaven! Give me over to the Eyes of Ra! Let me be bound to the Eyes of Ra! Let me be guided by the Eyes of Ra!

It is hard to recreate relationships that you let slip away.

32

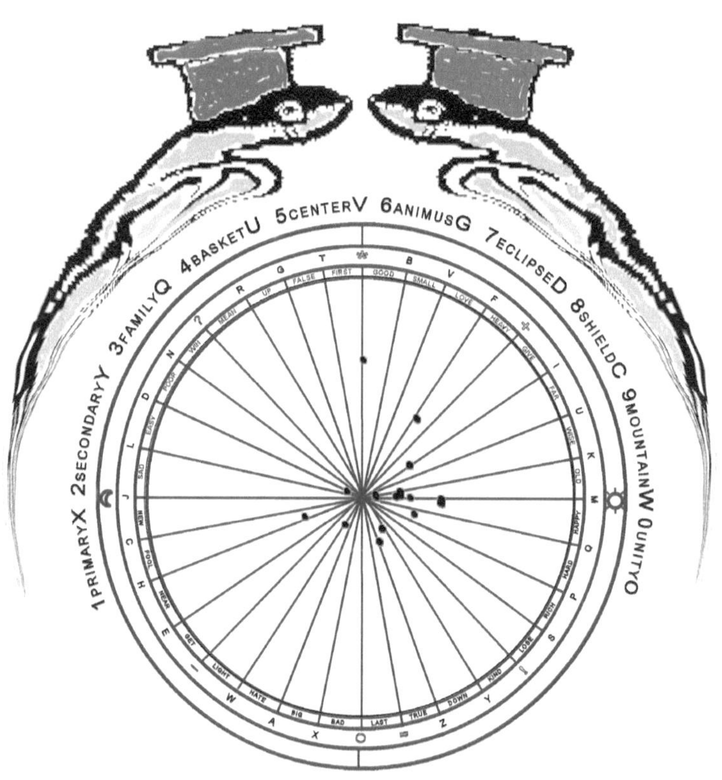

"You are a strong, confident and natural spiritual mystic force. Your active Mind is suspended between planes. There is a direct link between your Spirit and Body. This makes your Body a powerful weapon."

Love is the "flesh of the universe".

Painting with the colors of death.

33

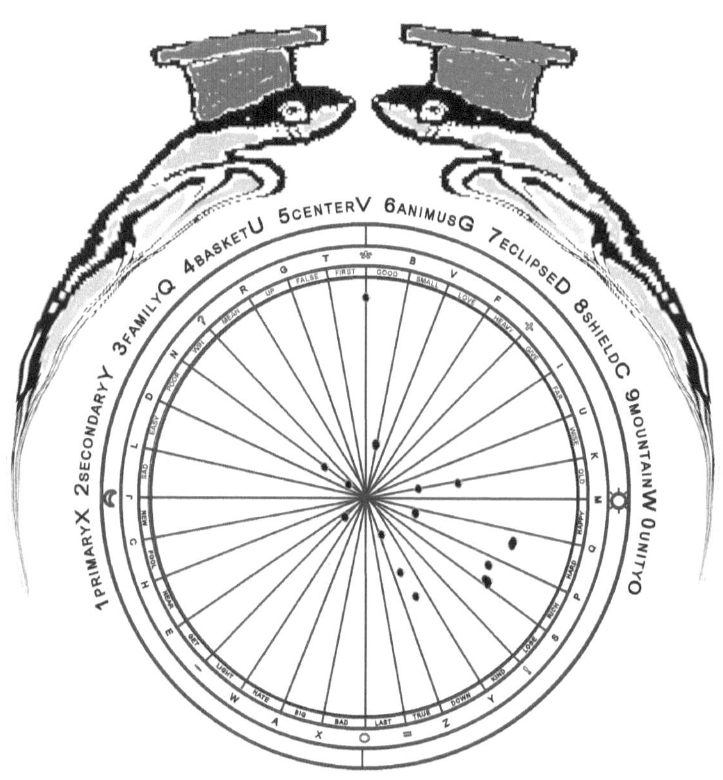

"The Spirit is forgetful and falling into sleep. The Mind is focused on the Body and increasing its strength by a private truth. The Body by this process becomes like a gem stone."

At the beginning of the Alchemical process you are bathed in the black.

There is a symbolic connection between the eye and a crystal. That is why we can "see" with crystals.

34

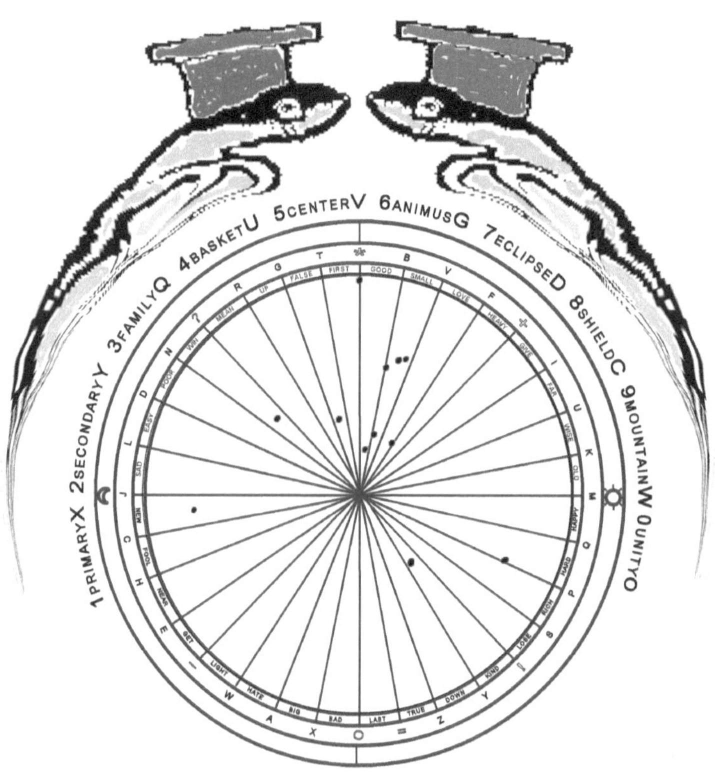

"You will uncover a deception and strike back to correct it. Your eyes have a new vision thanks to your growing psychic brain power."

Alchemical transformation is the acknowledgment that "being" refers to more than the Ego. "Being" is a we.

You are the Moon. Access to the divine feminine does not weaken your arm but tempers your blade. You are no longer blinded staring into the sun.

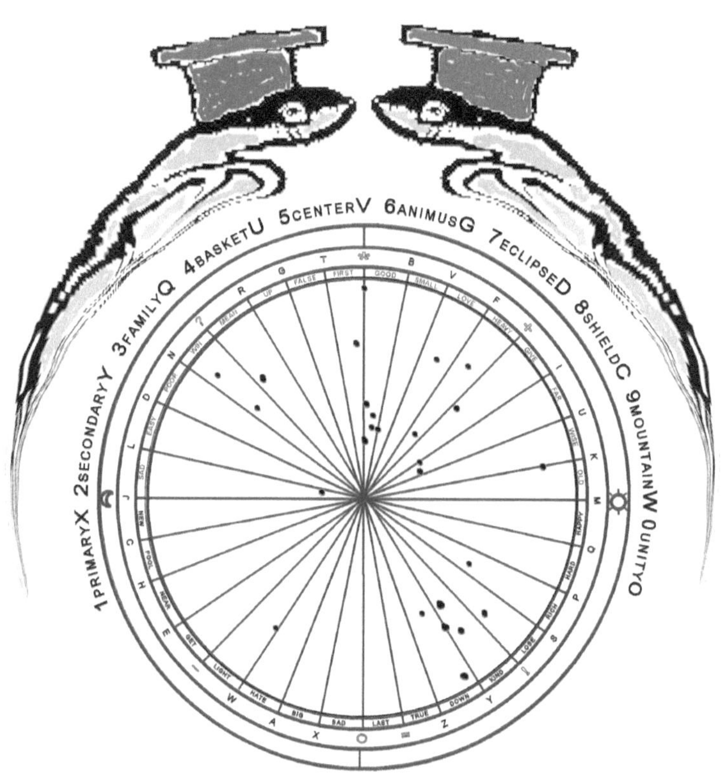

35

"Your deep Spirit is fed by a powerful secret creation of the Mind that is unconscious. Your Body is charged with disposing of the remaining and overflowing energy. The bodily cycle for this process is from anger to love and uncomfortable feelings to sensual joy."

Every day you shed your skin like a snake.

Always begin your work with an offering to the Eyes of Ra and a word of praise to Thoth. To mark the evolution of Sekhmet to Hathor pour a little wine into the sand.

36

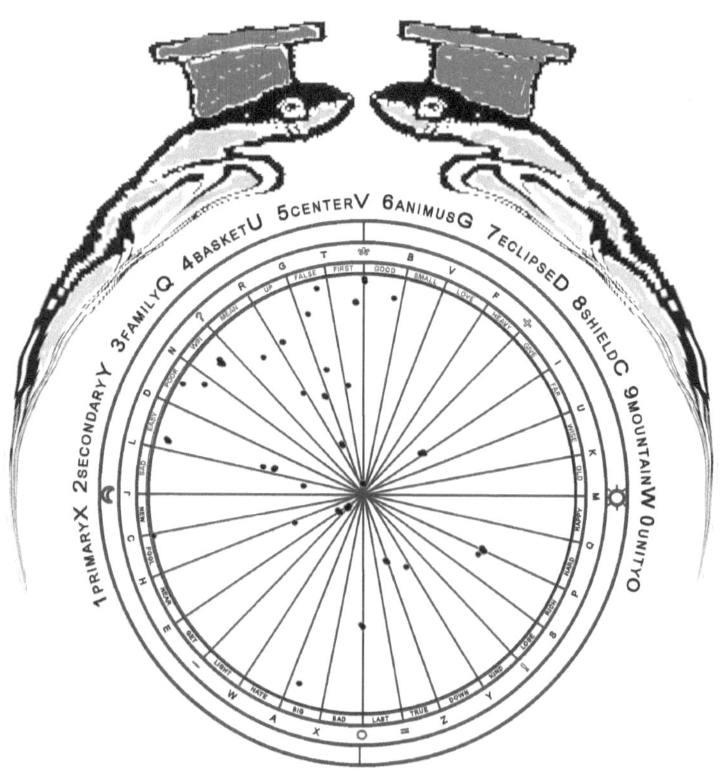

"You will receive good news from a written source. Your Mind is moving between Body and Spirit directing their activities. Directing Spirit seems easy at first but is a rewarding challenge. Your Body is solid and in good balance. You may wake in the night at times and this greatly increases your health as long as it's only a short time and you easily return to sleep."

Fire Khepr
Water Hathor
Air Thoth
Earth Osiris

If an idea resonates within you take it and use it. By using it you give thanks for it.

37

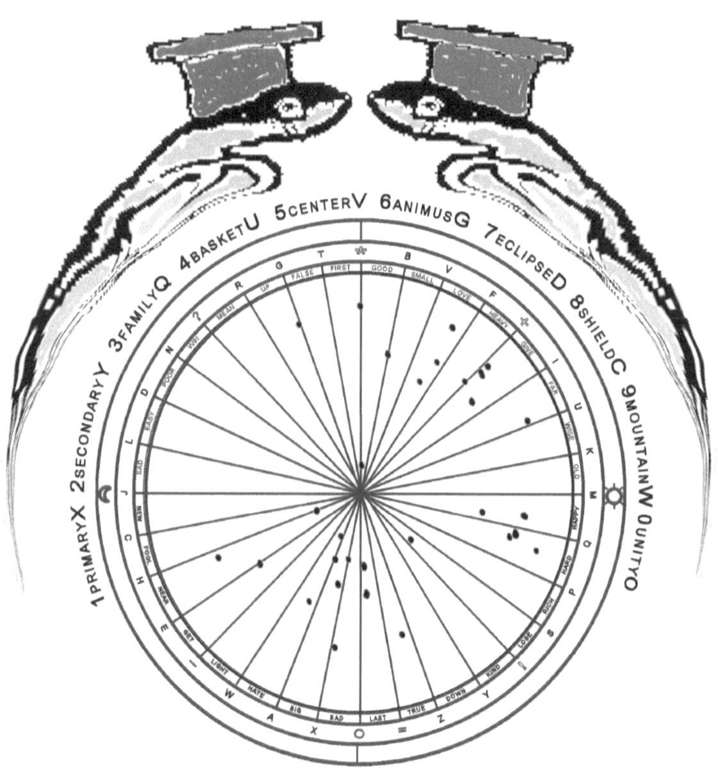

"You have regained your stability. The negative feelings from a past conflict are fading away. Your gifts are intense love and deception. Your attractions and desires should be written down and kept secret to empower your physical Body ensuring that the main object of desire cannot escape."

Thoughts are fire. Bones are earth. Blood- water. Breath- the air.

Praise them because you find the Goddesses within you. They don't want the worship of the powerless. They want all of you. Praise the Eyes of Ra!

38

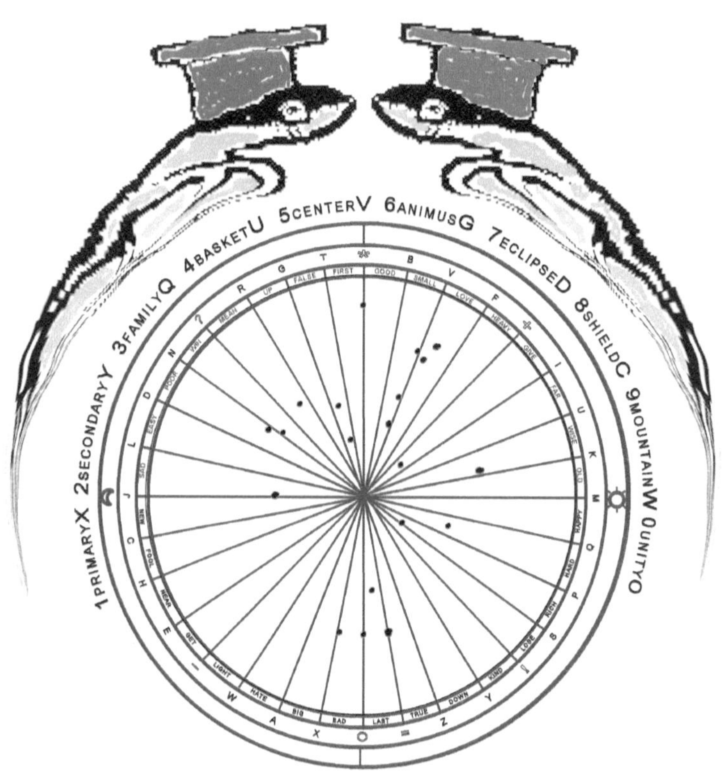

"You must concentrate and find the spiritual in you. You are awakening from a slumber of only Mind and Body. Your first attempts at this will fail. After a difficult trial you will find your path. Sexual activity is also a spiritual activity."

You opened your heart and the moonlight flooded its chambers.

Rebirth in Mercurialized Sulphur. An ego alloyed with the universal power.

39

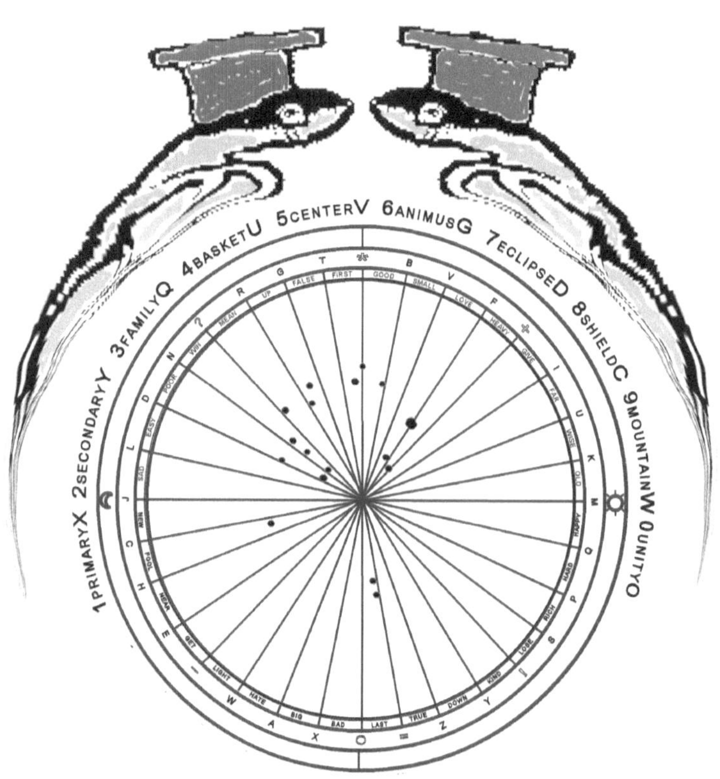

"*Your Spirit is under attack. The attack will succeed but the victory will be elusive to the attacker. You have escaped the heavy losses by hiding in the Mind and remaining silent, still and invisible. After the danger passes there will be a spiritual pain to overcome.*"

Cloaked in Redness like the Lady of Love.

A warning.

Drink too deep of truth and you drown.

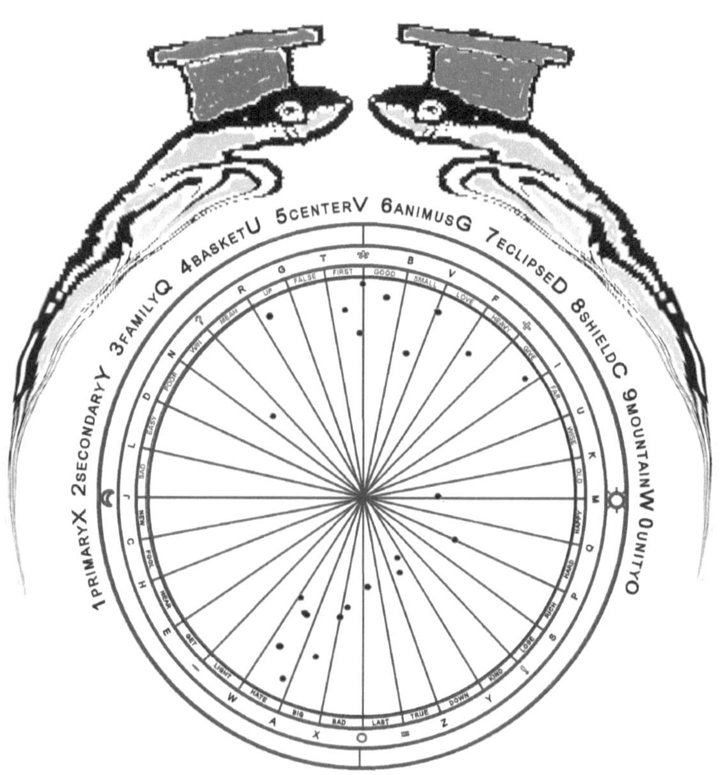

40

"You are a strong leader right now because you must be. You had a great idea before. Express it again. Recent changes to the Body related to the mouth or speech are not as beneficial as you believe."

Don't think her name while intoxicated--

We are attracted to opposites because we wish to commune with the unconscious.

41

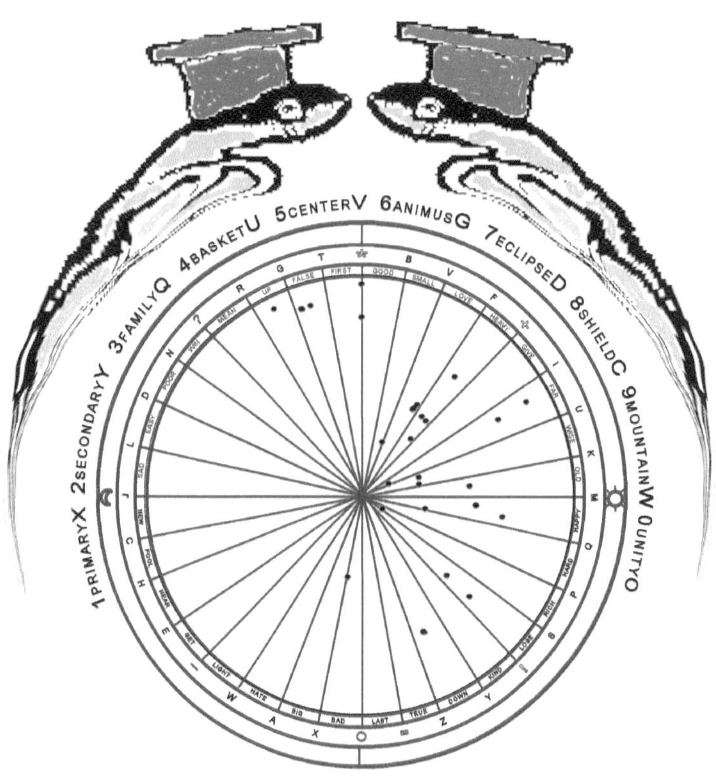

"You are always serious and deep in thought. But you are changing. The Feminine aspect is ascending with a centering on the family, loved ones and near responsibilities. This is a difficult transition. You liked having your head in the clouds but now the rain is falling."

I have become a cup.

What distinguishes Alchemy from commonplace spirituality is the final reintegration of the material into the spiritualized being. To descend back to the body renewed and fortified completes the great work.

42

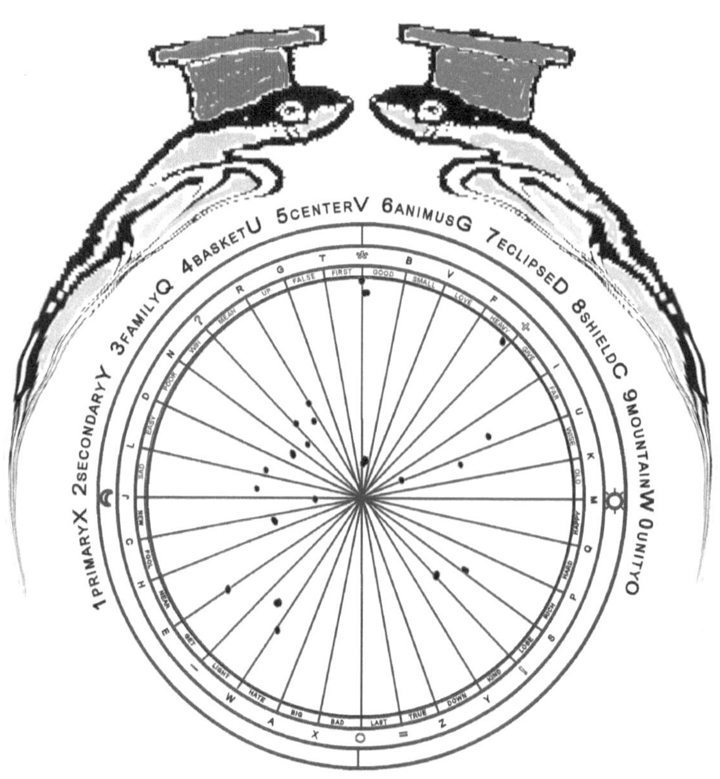

"You find a difficult solution to a simple problem. The solution makes you unhappy but it is for the best. You are physically tired and mentally spent after your discovery. Put the idea in writing and say it aloud to activate it and refresh yourself."

You have taken on many names because you have many faces.

Where they once used fire you can use electricity. Where they once used heat you can use light.

43

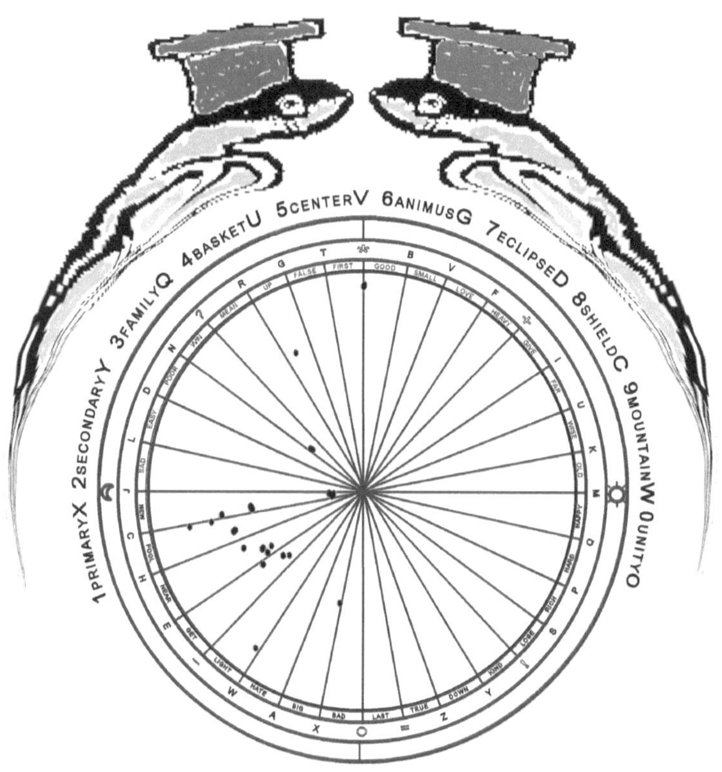

"Your Body and Mind are working together to safely bring about a new spiritual self. You are creating your own set of rules. You are taking in the energy and converting it to a material form of light."

Mother Lover Daughter Wife

I am the Water of Life

I am the River of Life

The Divine Feminine guides your spiritual transformation. Every day you have a more comprehensive view of yourself and your place in the cosmos. You find yourself able to see through the eyes of others. Your ego is welcoming. You are becoming pure.

44

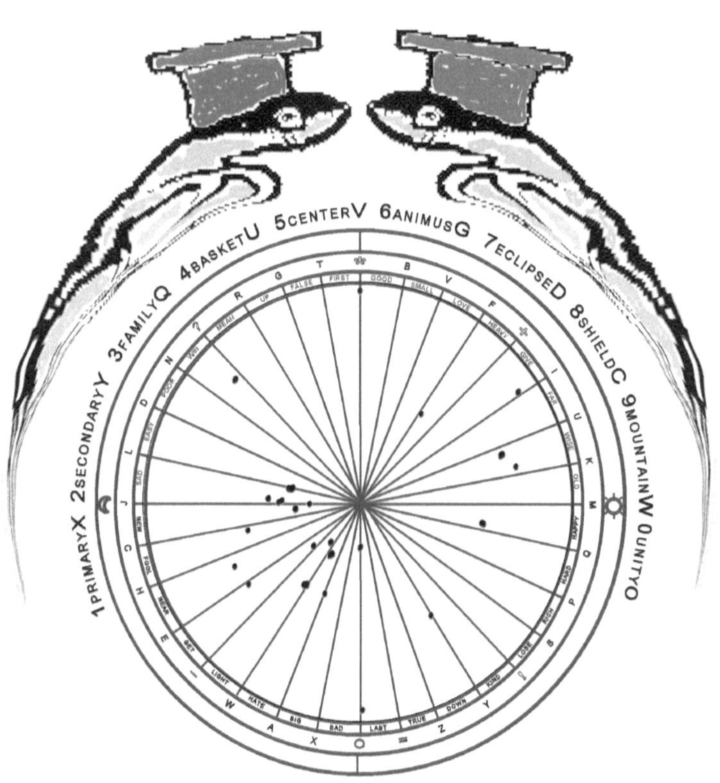

"You are in need of cleansing. You must make a sacrifice in a valley. Follow these instructions and keep your power at the ready. Your Body is strong. You will prevail. Pleasure and wisdom come from the Body."

Strip down in the hot sun. Find a refreshing pool and laughing bodies.

Copper is an equivalent of Sulphur. Also the Red Lion.

45

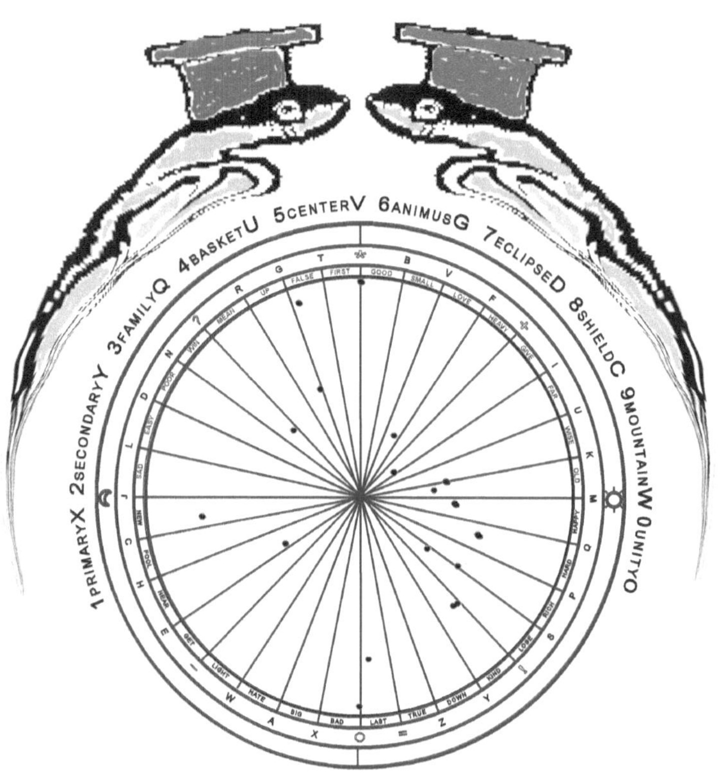

"You will undertake a heroic adventure to reclaim something or someone you have loved in the past. Question your senses and actions when the task becomes difficult."

When patience runs dry-

slake the thirst with excess.

If Sekhmet's breath is the desert then her voice is
the sun.

46

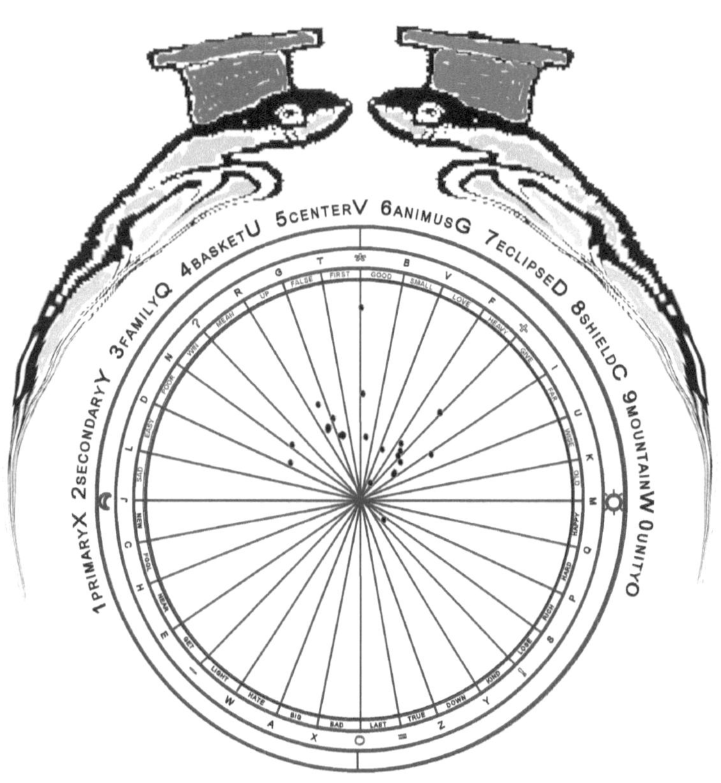

"Be warned. You will lose a spiritual attack. You will need to concentrate intensely to defend yourself as best you can to minimize the damage and heal."

The New Moon Evocation:

The stone takes into its heart

The soul of the one who will take part

Be it for healthy life or painful death

The soul is bound from them to itself

I call on Menhit's awesome power

And the love of Hathor in this hour

To guide the soul across timeless space

Into the stone to take its place

Internalize the Goddesses and your spirit is their domain. Bless the Eyes of Ra!

47

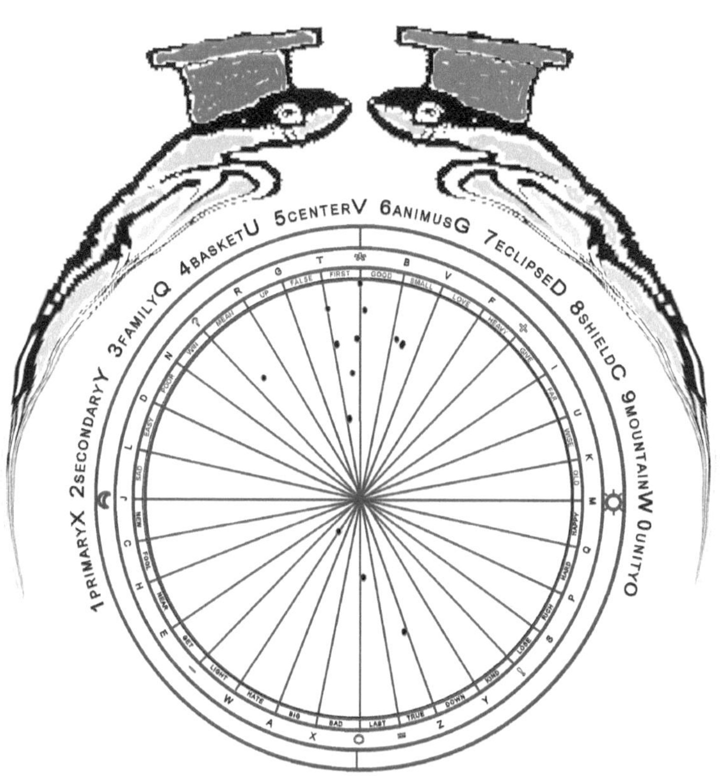

"At the time of death, thoughts will split into many small pieces and enter into the Spirit."

Full Moon Evocation:

As the Moon is full of cosmic soul

The stone brims with symbols stole'

Reaped from an empty vessel now overflowing

with crystalline will begins the sowing

The death of the ego is the path of transformation.

48

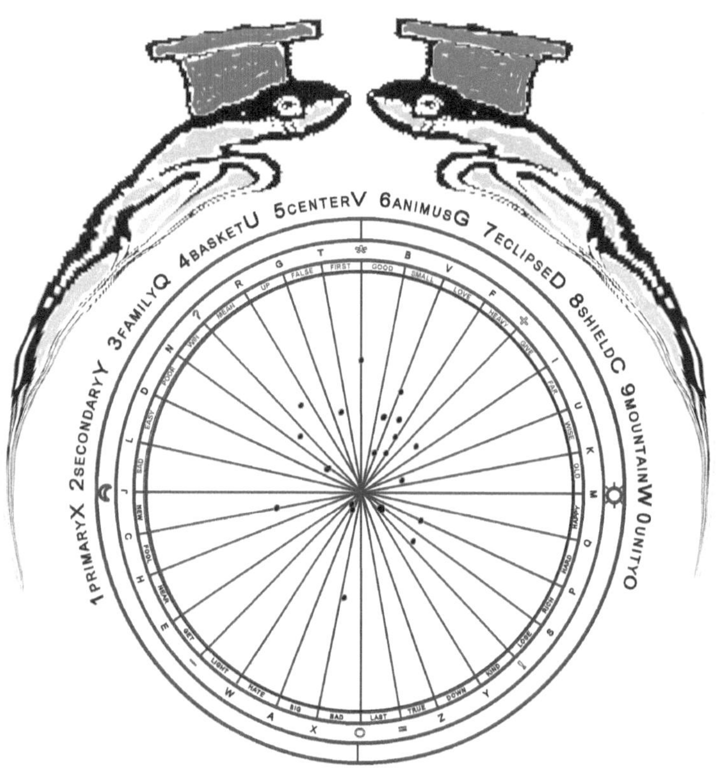

"Your power comes from the dark night. You are making a plan to protect yourself against wasting your love on the undeserving."

Binding Evocation:

To bind this deal I make the seal, let the hands be tied

Into the light or darkest night, The Eyes of Ra abide

The soul held fast to sacred stone awaits their divine gaze

Until such time as the seal is broke and it returns from whence it came

Your everyday self has great value. The starting point, the prima materia, the black sun. There can be no transformation without a point of ascension. And when you return, you will warmly embrace that Saturnian self.

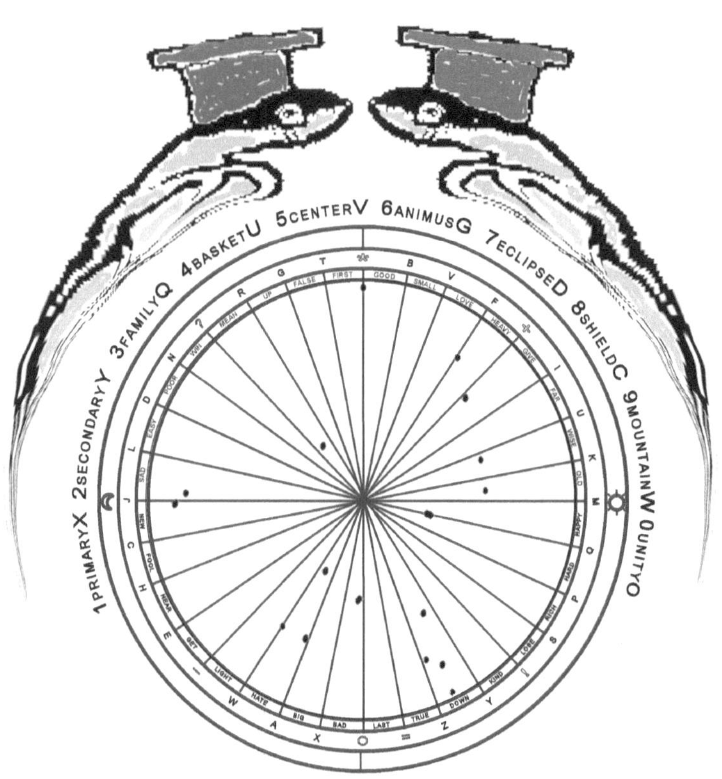

"*You are giving yourself to others like a Father. With your physical Body you wage war for others. You must act on instinct and give up grand goals and ideas.*"

At the full moon you are Min, at the new moon, Saturn.

The calculation of probability is the most important skill. The capacity for love is the most important character trait. The healthy nutritive system is the most important biological function.

50

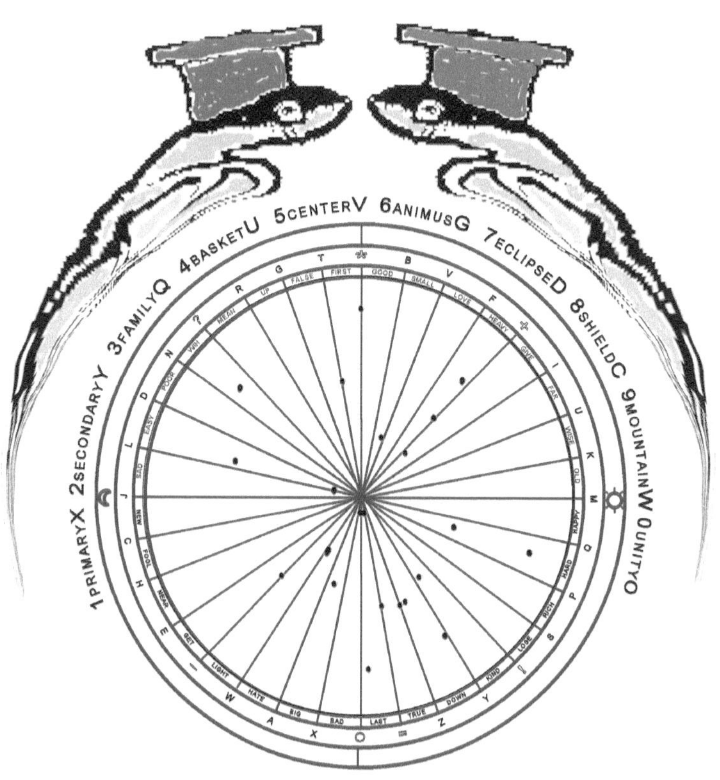

"You are grounded by your Spirit and your physical Body has corresponding ethereal properties. Your Mind is accordingly supple and travels between the three planes with ease although it is more difficult to return to the Body."

The divine feminine is not moved by the transitory.

Alchemists use physical materials to both symbolize and activate a spiritual transformation. The
goal is to merge oneself with the universal spirit.

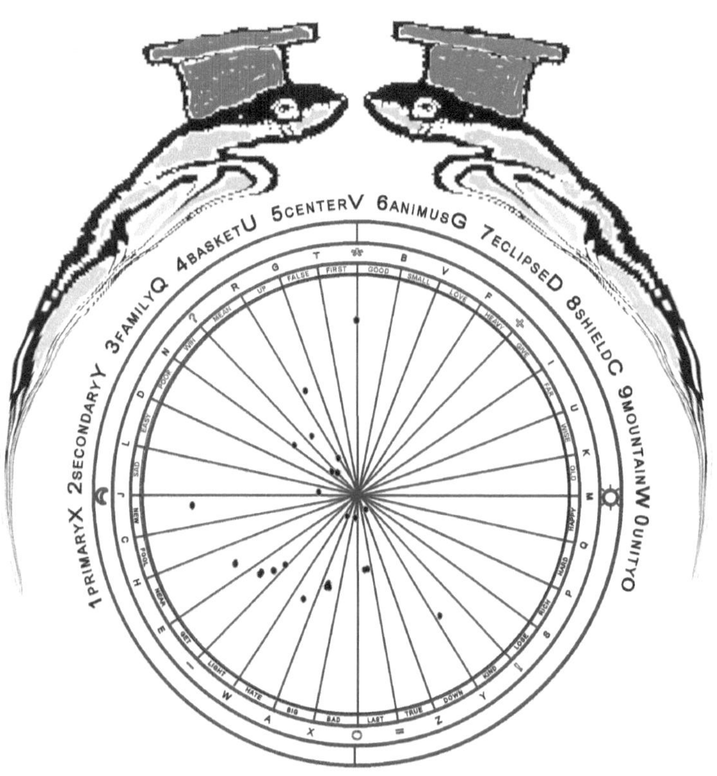

51

"There is a divine presence in your Spirit with you. It was sleeping within you but has awoken. It is cleansing and fortifying your Spirit. It is heat and Fire. You will receive a final and dangerous piece of knowledge to integrate the presence within you. There will also be a dramatic change to your physical Body."

The evolution of the spirit is mirrored in the evolution of the Goddess.

Blackening - Analysis

Whitening - Catalysis

Reddening - Synthesis

52

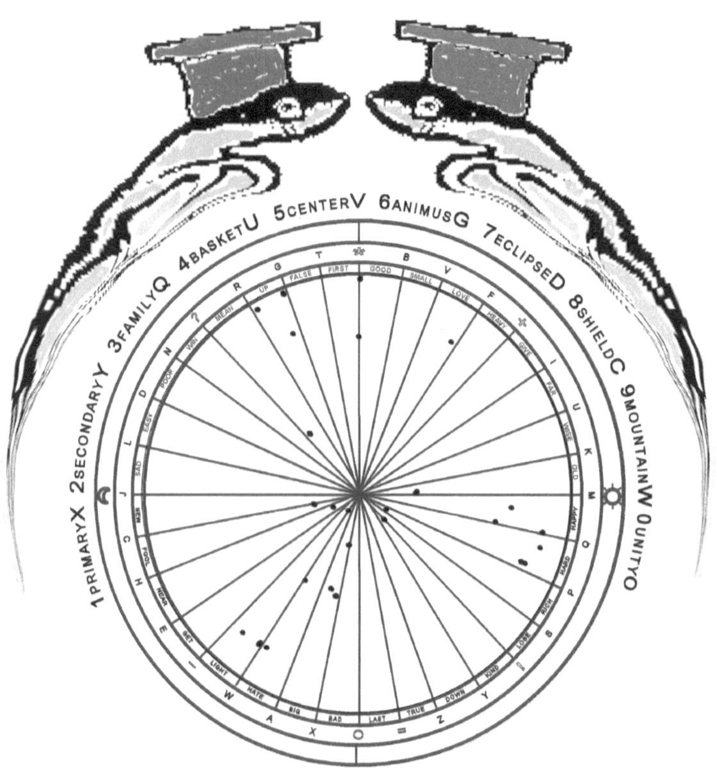

"Your Spirit is your home, wealth and great protector of your family. Your Mind is magically and joyfully active in supporting the Spirit in its work. Your physical Body performs stiff movements dedicated to the Spirit as in dance. The movements are pleasurable and take place in darkness."

To have it all and still crave transformation: That is alchemy.

The Moon is an aspect of the transformative agency.

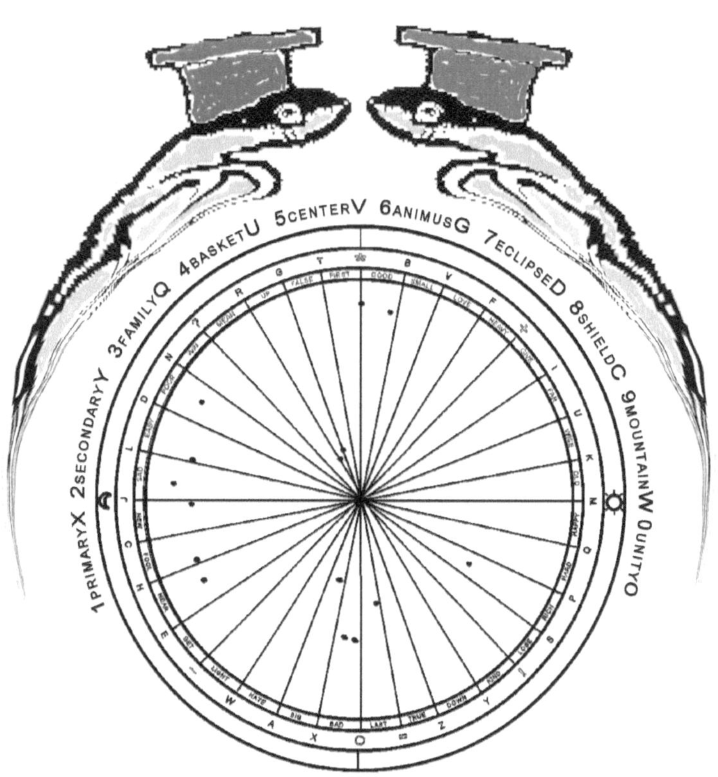

"There is revealed a significant sign or vision related to your soul status. There is a change coming. A transition from the mental to the physical plane that will be uncomfortable at first. The outcome will be positive after time. Distract yourself temporarily from the fixation on wealth."

There is nothing more inspiring than a beautiful body.

Dr. Woodruff 17 MAR 1929 (Sun)-

Started construction of electrical sparking apparatus. It is meant "to test the effect of the sparks and high tension currents and electrical and roentgen rays on different materials".

54

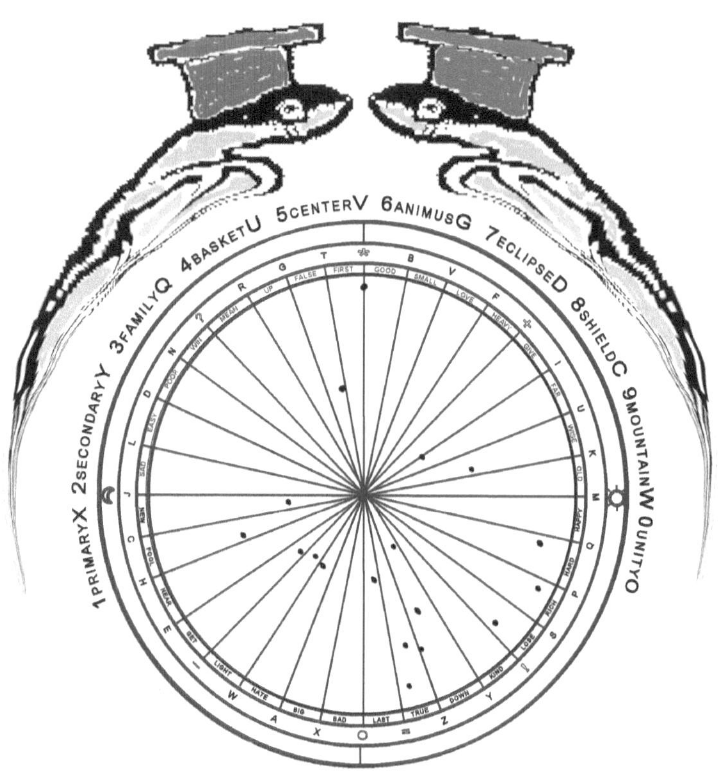

"You are confident. You have experienced a shift from spiritual towards more mental and physical energies. This is overall a positive change but there are some vexing intellectual challenges ahead. You have greatly increased strength at the cost of some dexterity which is augmented by advanced sexual power in the mental plane."

When you are transformed the world around you is also transformed.

Dr. Woodruff 18 MAR 1929 (Mon)-

Completed connections of the electrical apparatus. This causes current as at low pressure to be transformed to pressure so great that a gap of three centimeters of conductivity wire is bridged- Sparks come across the gap; they are blue-violet in color.

55

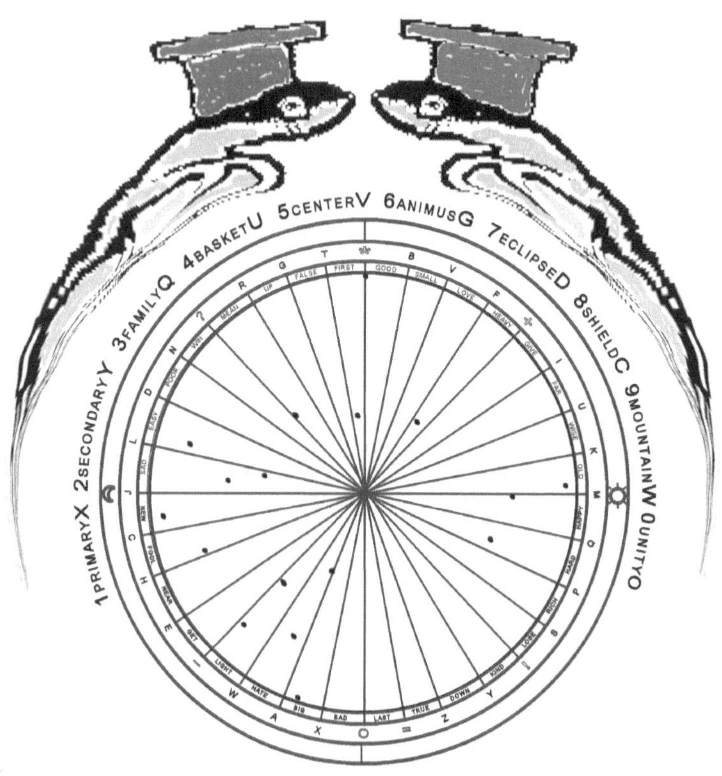

"The Female energies are forcefully emerging through a formerly Male dominated energy core. The reason this is happening is unknown, but the response will be vigorous. The resulting change will turn out to be very pleasant and satisfying."

Meeting the Unconscious is transformative.

Dr. Woodruff 19 MAR 1929 (Tue)-

By similar treatment crystals of Acetamide which are transparent, formed a white solid and by continuous treatment a substance black like that I mentioned before was formed, however I did not test the soluability of this substance in aqueus Potassium Hydroxide. Heating merely melts the crystals which form needle like crystals unlike the substance mentioned above.

56

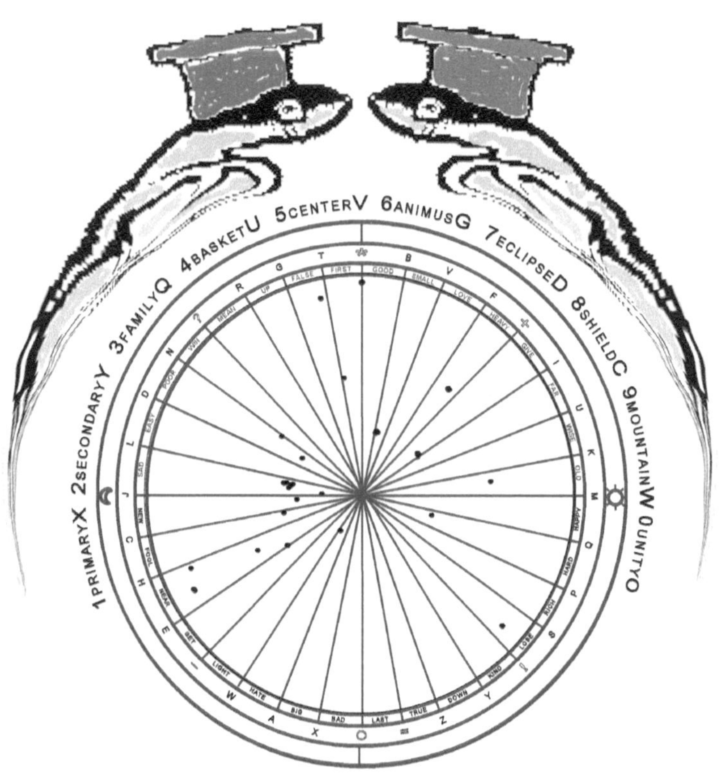

"You are a sacred guardian winding down a significant work. There will be a transition to another phase that will be more important to your spiritual development and is related to a familiar tradition. This involves a technical change to your habits or practice."

When you see a closed door assume you can open it.

Dr. Woodruff 19 MAR 1929 (Tue)-

No heating on these substances was noted through the electrical application.

57

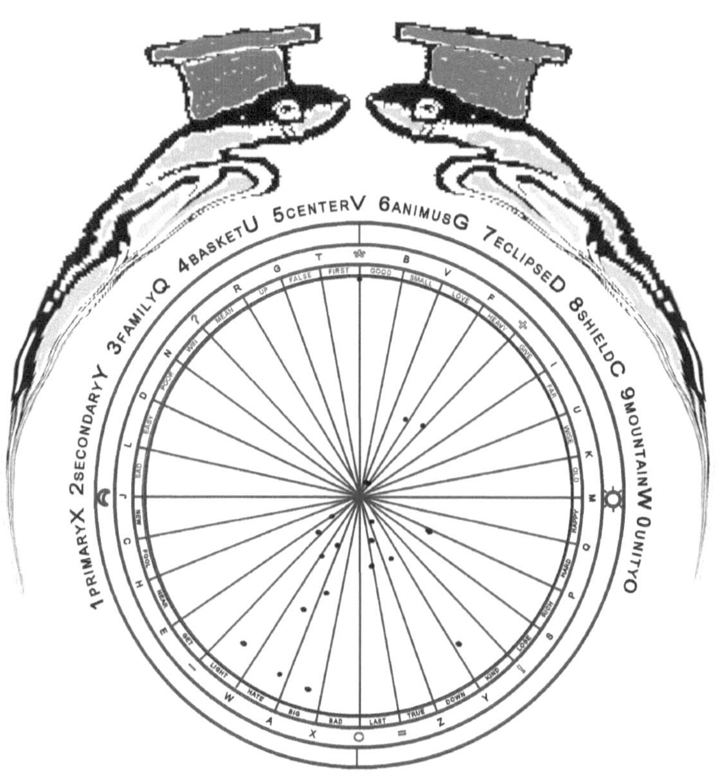

"There are powerful words of love at the center of your Spirit that permeate your Mind and Body. Say these words aloud confidently to push down the negative thoughts as they occur. As you say these words you must smile or laugh in a kindly fashion."

A feminine energy whispers. Was it a spirit guide or your own unconscious?

Dr. Woodruff 20 MAR 1929 (Wed)-

By the action of the long blue sparks on Potassium Chlorate is produced a black substance similar to that mentioned March 19. I could not produce a black substance by heating more of this compound.

58

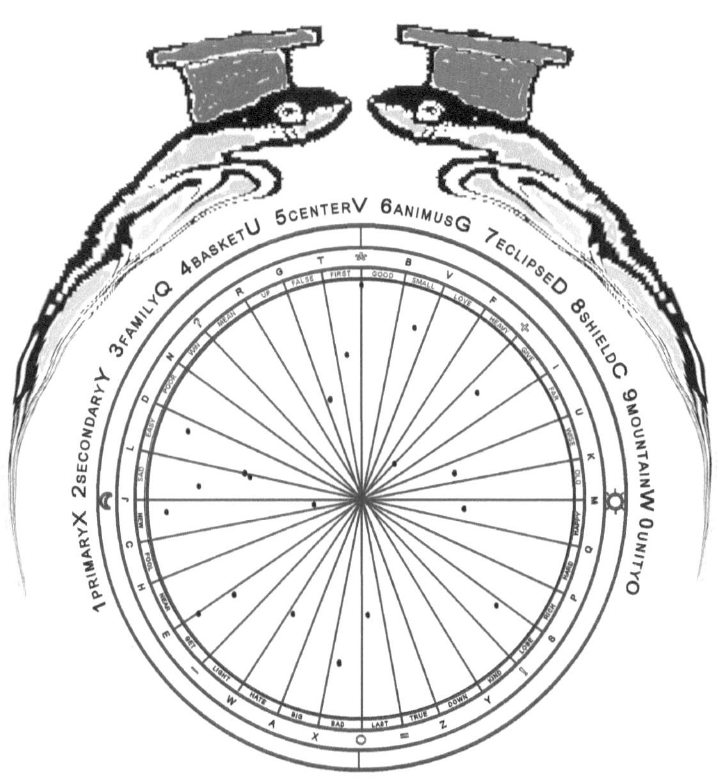

"There is firm double support for a new project or plan. The planes reveal the dynamics of this. A Mind change to an earlier state has released you from a petty annoyance and liberated new spiritual energy and a new physical skill."

Transform yourself so that society bends around you.

Dr. Woodruff 20 MAR 1929 (Wed)-

The action of the spark-series upon Stannic Chloride Hydrate only melted the crystals and when allowed to cool bubbles formed and the melted crystals became solid. No black substance was observed which could be differentiated from the brown produced on the Iorn plate by the compound. I feel that my method was at fault; that some substance conductive should be used as a baci in place of the Iorn corroded by the Stannic Chloride. The method was satisfactory in former tests because napthol, Acetamide, or Chlorate of Potash caused erosion of the plate of Iorn.

59

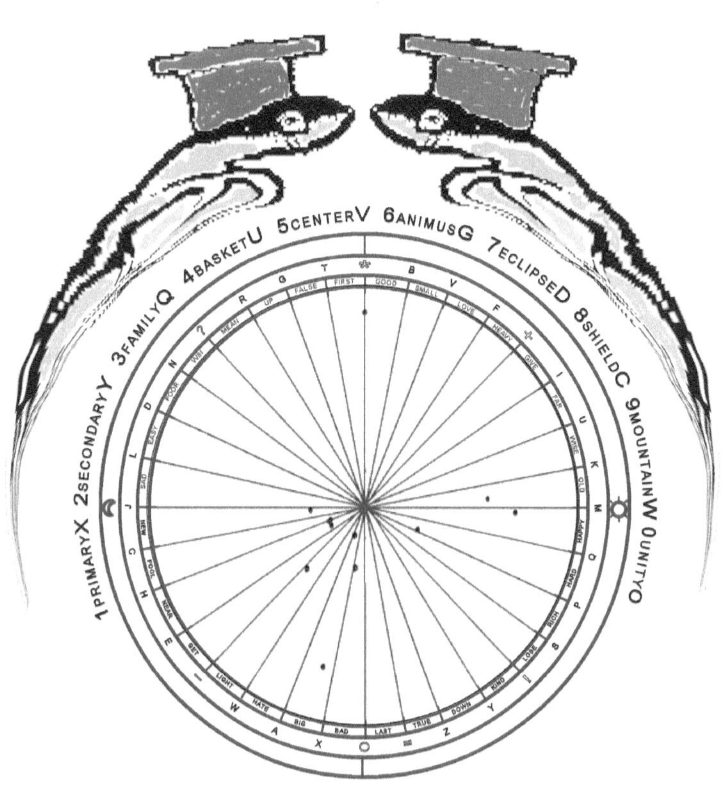

"Someone is occupying you. You are convinced in spite of doubts that a sacrifice is needed to renew your bond with that person which will in turn connect you with a cherished symbol from the past that you are in need of and will give you intense pleasure."

People are the most beautiful gifts.

Dr. Woodruff 21 MAR 1929 (Th)-

Reduced Copper Oxide to metallic Copper by heating in a current of Hydrogen.

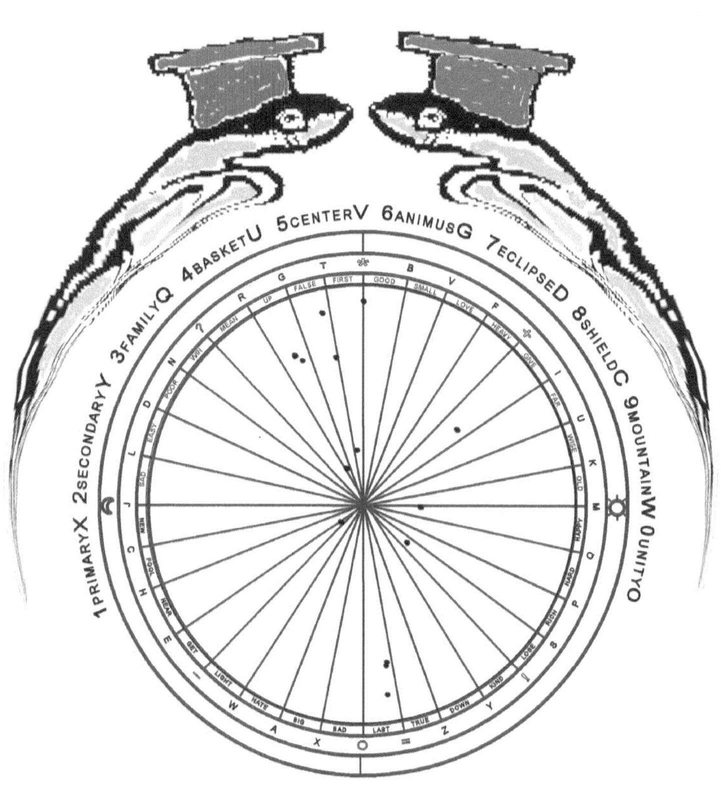

"You have achieved an important milestone in the mental plane. Don't diminish that by taking on new spiritual tasks right now. You are spiritually in a charging phase, but you need to assist someone to bring it to fruition. You are in a practical mood and are distracted by a bodily issue, but it is not serious."

Where and in whom shall we meet?

Dr. Woodruff 21 MAR 1929 (Th)-

Resorcinol forms a dark colored substance as does Potassium Dichromate when treated by the sparks mentioned March 20. It is striking that an inorganic compound should form a substance so much like Carbon to the eye. Let the Resorcinol and other substances formed, if any, remain in contact with Potassium Hydroxide Solution.

61

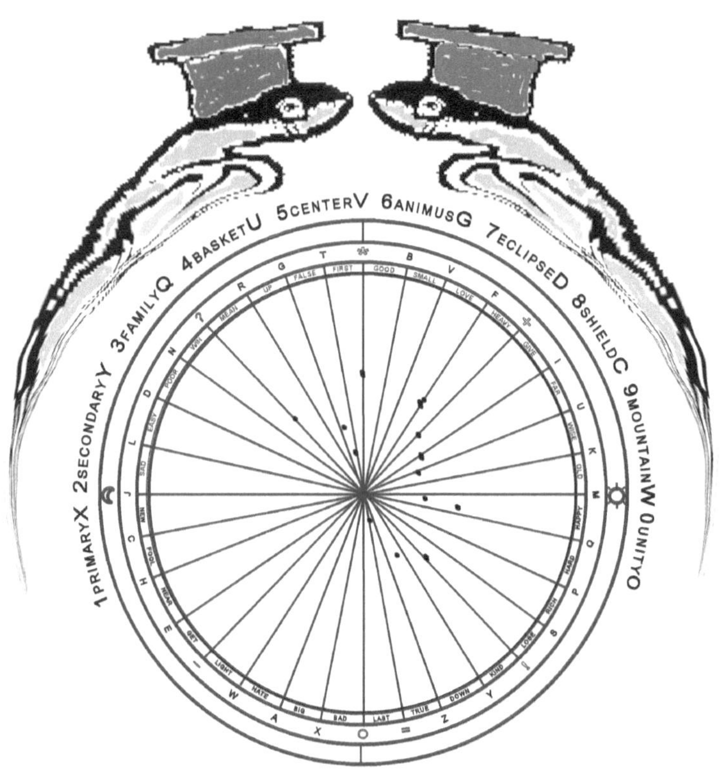

"You completed a plane transition recently, but during that time you were targeted by someone for a psychic attack. You will have to intuit your battle plan because thinking it over isn't helping. Meditate on what makes you happy and you will break up the attack. You will conquer the lie."

Create for yourself a personal symbol and make it appear everywhere.

Dr. Woodruff 22 MAR 1929 (Fri)-

The Resorcinol and substances mentioned March 21 have a distinct greenish color much like that of nitroso-resorcinol. I accordingly treated with acid to see if it formed a red solution as does nitroseresorcinol. I find that it does. The only place where nitrogen could come from to form this would be the atmosphere. Treated alpha napthol with the same kind of long spark and let the product remain in contact with the Aqueus Potassium Hydroxide. The observation of the result will be made some future date.

62

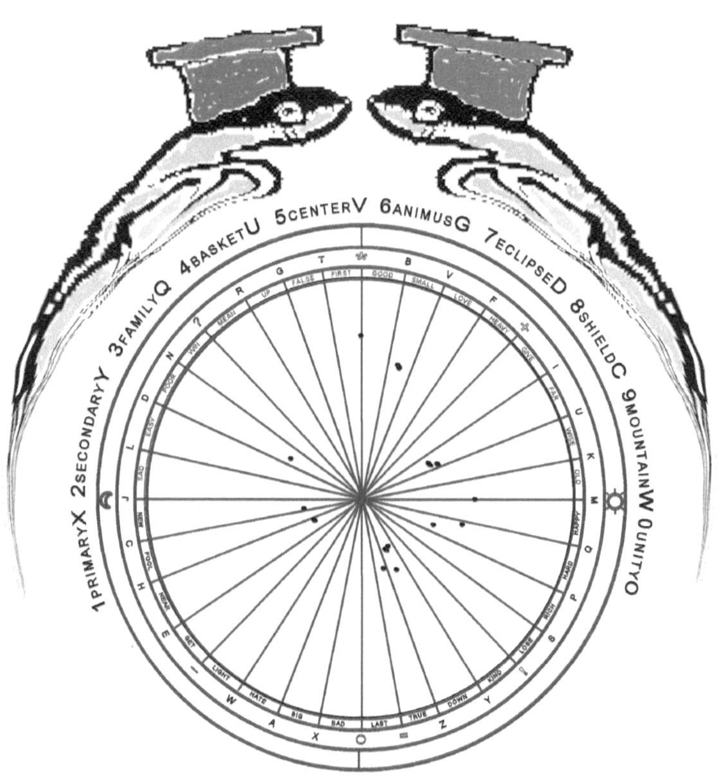

"You are protected in your position between planes during integration. It is a difficult mental feat, and you are pulled toward the physical plane against your will. You have to concentrate on a distant goal that looks insignificant at the moment. Your success will strengthen you and will help you to assist someone. Arrange symbols for a clue."

If everything around you seems insignificant then you are transforming.

Dr. Woodruff 31 MAR 1929 (Sun)-

Prepared an alloy of Tin, Lead and Thorium. This is malleable. I beat it into a plate and cut into wire.

63

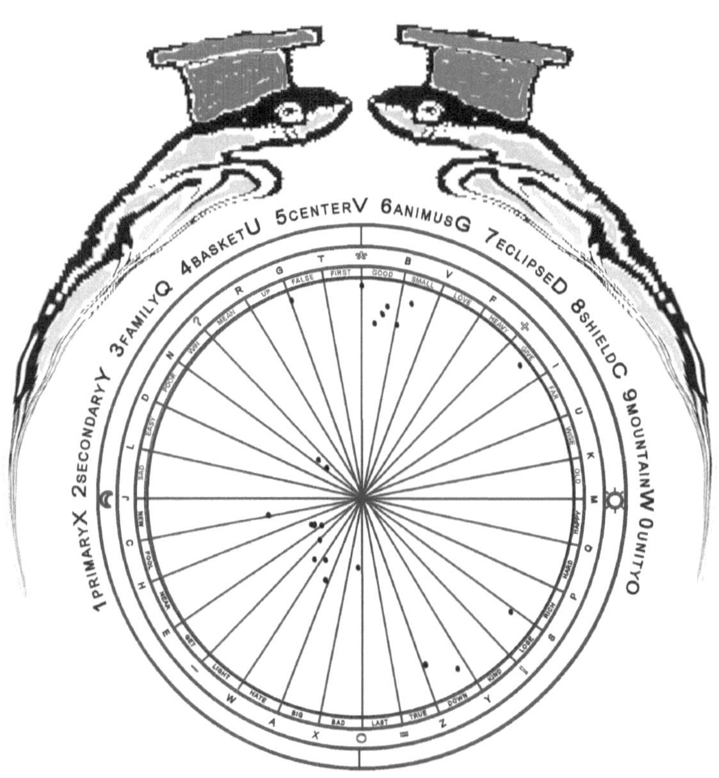

"This is health related. Your Mind is engaged in fighting an injury or illness. There is something that is shrinking due to your power over it. Your inner light (scepter) is focused through the Fire element to the adjoining physical plane burning the growth or tumor. Revealed 'leg' or 'walking' symbols refer to the waning of the injury."

To be cleansed by hot desert winds.

Dr. Woodruff 02 APRIL 1929 (Tue)-

Prepared an alloy of Thorium and Iorn by the electrolytic deposition of Thorium upon a Ferric plate and by subsequent heating.

64

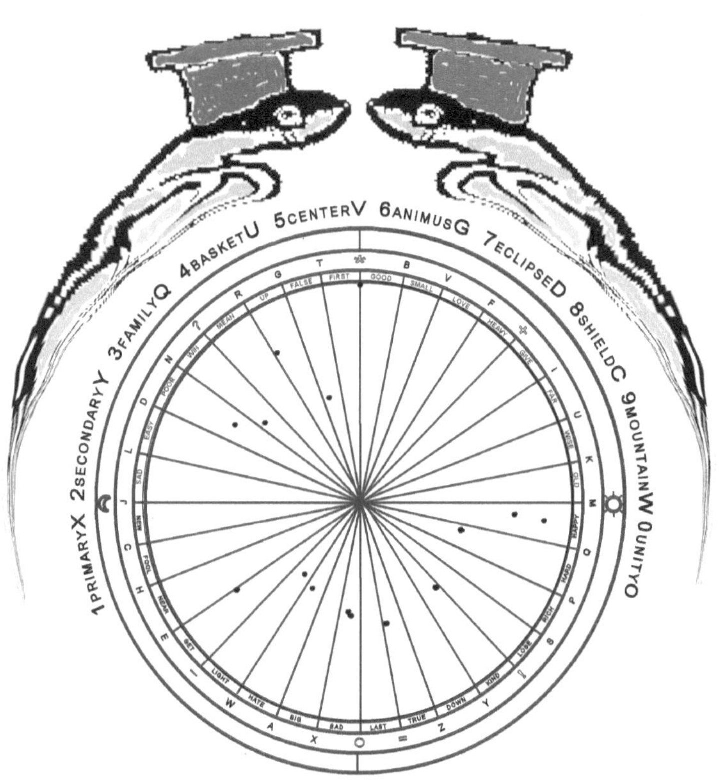

"You have decided it is wrong to carry a severe negative feeling and a spiritual / medical book is calling you that offers help. The advice will be very effective and verbally oriented causing joy to replace the negativity, but at some small cost."

Be devoted to the Goddesses because they are part of you.

Dr. Woodruff 02 APRIL 1929 (Tue)-

Placed both plates, not touching in a solution of Thorium nitrate and Hydrochloric Acid. Connected the wires mentioned March 31 between the two plates but without the solution, with the welding of all joints. No reactions except bubbling on plates. When the wire is severed and Thorium nitrate placed in the opening, no reaction occurs.

65

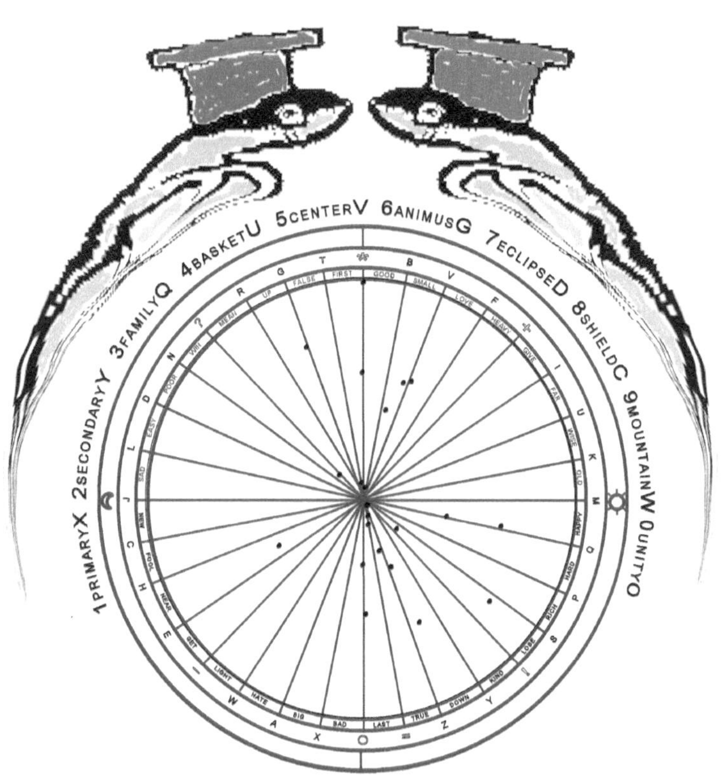

"You have recently had an intense spiritual event that is over or near the end. You are about to shift emphasis to practical concerns involving care for family and career matters. Your Body is aligned with these goals and you have strength at your command. Your balance and focus are excellent."

Find the treasure within yourself and then give it all away.

Dr. Woodruff 04 APRIL 1929 (Th)-

Passed the sparks mentioned March 18 between the electrodes of the Lead, Tin, Thorium alloy of March 31. Noticed no abnormal action. Passed the spark through a tube nearly empty of air. A blue-green light was observed on the side of the tube. A small piece of carbohydrate put near this tube vibrates somewhat. Directed the spark of March 18 upon some Thorium nitrate. The white oxide formed which gave off a bright light.

(Last mention of the Apparatus)

66

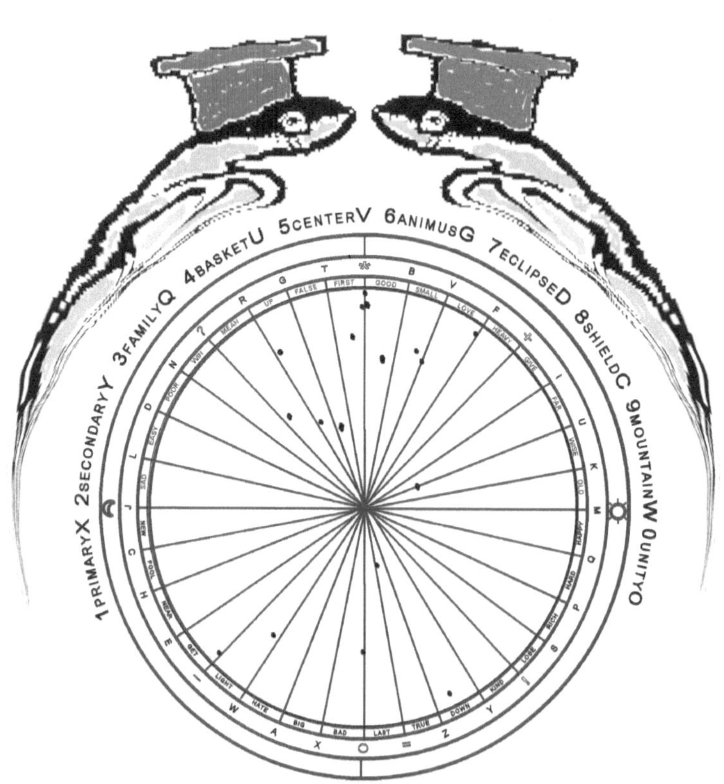

"*Integrated Feminine energy is a principle of movement through the planes. Mental focus is powerful but not so much on the desired spiritual target. You received a specific hand sign to defend from imminent hostile Spirit action.*"

NNT	**(water)**	1 1 1
NN	**(water)**	-1 -1 -1
AMNT	**(obscurity)**	-1 1 1
AMN	**(obscurity)**	1 -1 -1
KKT	**(darkness)**	-1 -1 1
KK	**(darkness)**	1 1 -1
HHT	**(infinity)**	1 -1 1
HH	**(infinity)**	-1 1 -1

Niger Sol- The Black Sun

The part of our will that is hidden from ourselves. The body acts autonomously under its direction. Beware its appetites. It tends to eat itself if not fed properly.

67

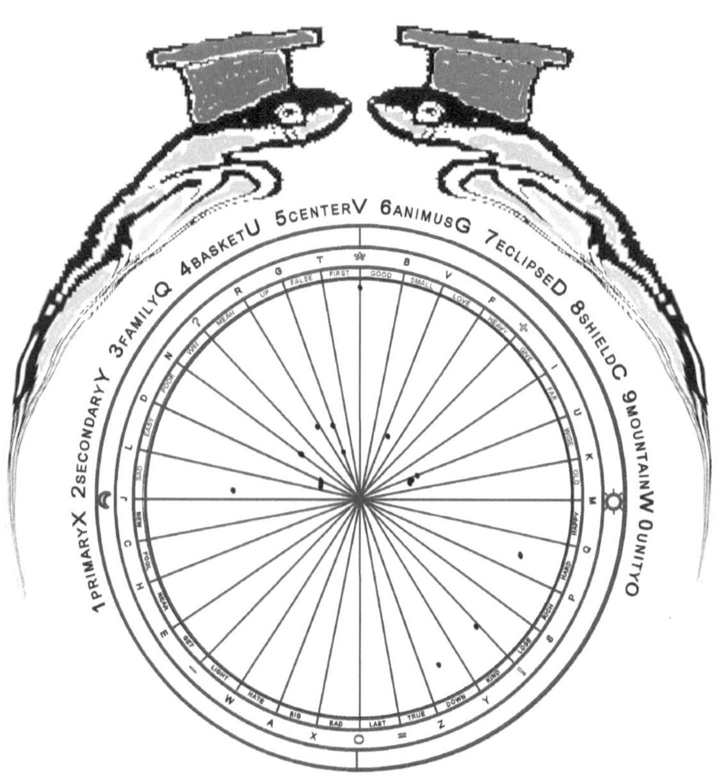

"Spiritually your protection is a strong immovable character that comes naturally to you. Mentally you are either considering motherhood, or other profound, creative events. You are verbally expressing these thoughts but sometimes forgetting to realize them. Physically, your Body is asking for attention. Especially to a toughness or stiffness in the lower Body."

Interpretations:

NNT/NN – water, water of life, newly differentiated matter, blood, mother, all, Mercury

KKT/KK - earth, black earth, shadow, Saturn, weight, objectivity, father, place, death, peace, time

AMNT/AMN – air, loss, distance, hidden, invisibility, flight, space, travel, Mars, sky, wind

HHT/HH – light, fire, forever, ego, will, passion, love, pain, alone, power, Venus

Spirit is the molecules moving through you. It is the synapses firing between neurons. You are the four elements.

68

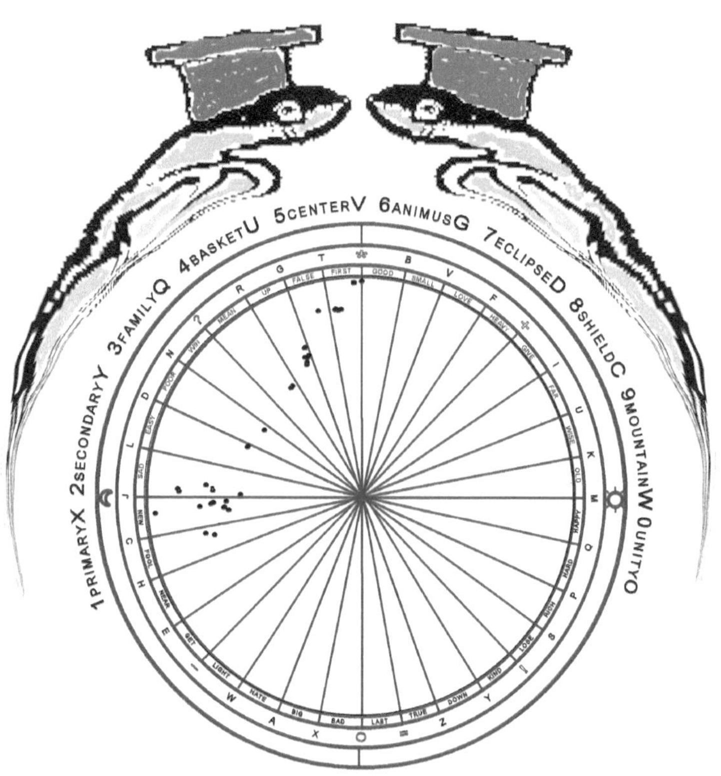

"*Weakness in the spiritual plane indicates that conscious activity dominates. A decision has been reached to shift from active willing to accepting and interpreting. The challenge is that you are not pleased with the ideas you are initially getting from outside. On the physical plane you are experiencing a new pain or displeasure but it's not what you think it is. Pay attention to signals from the Body.*"

Cross relations:

Dark Waters – Chaos (freedom)

Infinite Obscurity – Necessity (obedience)

With differentiation of internal mass, rotation can begin around a central axis.

69

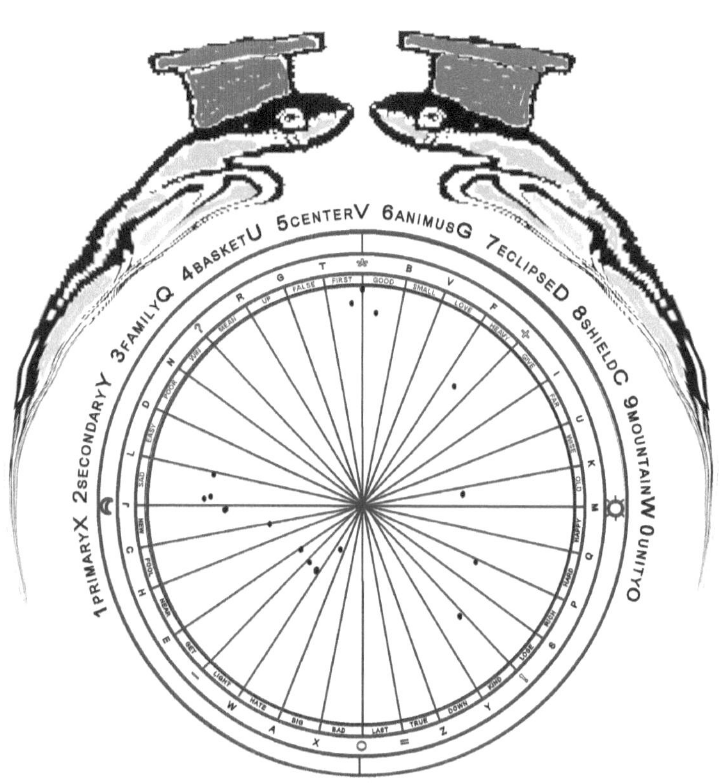

"The Spirit is troubled by negative energy. But the Mind with the help of the 'Old One', maybe a relative or ancestor, is battling with you. Great physical health is channeling fiery energy inward to the force of the Mind to drive out the negative energy. There is no resolution to the conflict yet."

Adjacent relations:

Invisible Waters – Life Force (love/sex)

Infinite Waters – Energy (movement/change)

Invisible Darkness – Matter (stillness/duration)

Infinite Darkness – Death Force (violence/war)

When she touches you the heart strings vibrate.

70

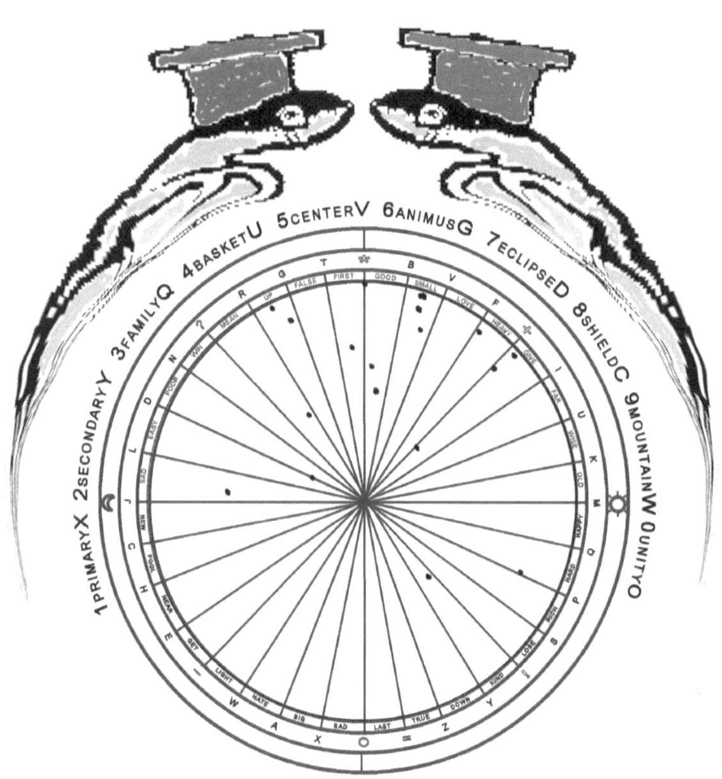

"*The Spirit is weakened. Fire is lacking. The Mind has been forced to re-align and assist the will. The Body is channeling energy through the portion of the brain that emits psychic energy. This process is the reason for the mental attitude changes. The goal is to heal the spiritual decline by self-giving. Symbolic affirmations indicate a successful outcome.*"

Existence requires asymmetry / heterogeneity.

Hathor chooses you. You cannot choose her. Some symbols are appropriate and some are not. The transcendent informs culture and culture does not form the transcendent.

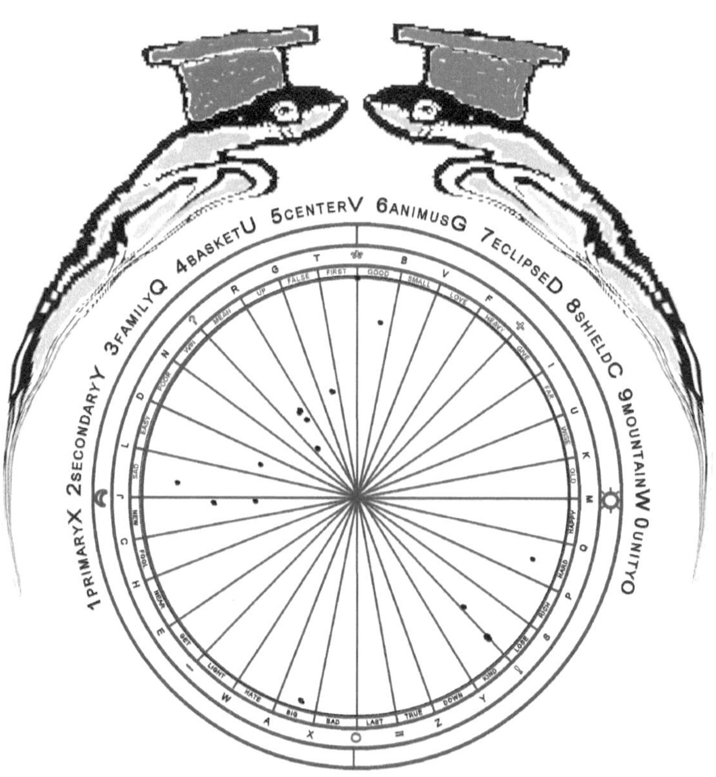

"The Air element presence means your intellectual powers are in the ascendant. Earth and Fire power are present to a lesser degree. There is a deficit in the Water element. Feelings of trust and safety are lacking. There is a spiritual or psychic pause."

It is not punishment if you like it.

The Nigredo, or blackening, is Analysis. Energy is applied. The material is reduced to constituent parts and examined.

72

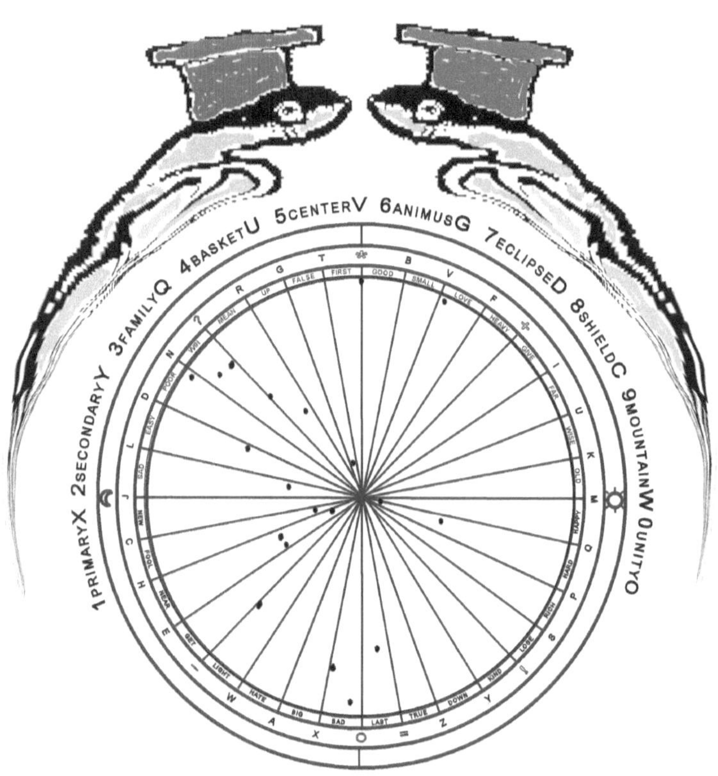

"You are overcoming spiritual errors with the power of family blood and by the composition of the Body. Your sex life may be disrupted during the transition from error to truth which will have difficult moments."

If you cannot make something of yourself, make something out of someone else.

Alchemy takes a refined perception and a restless will.

73

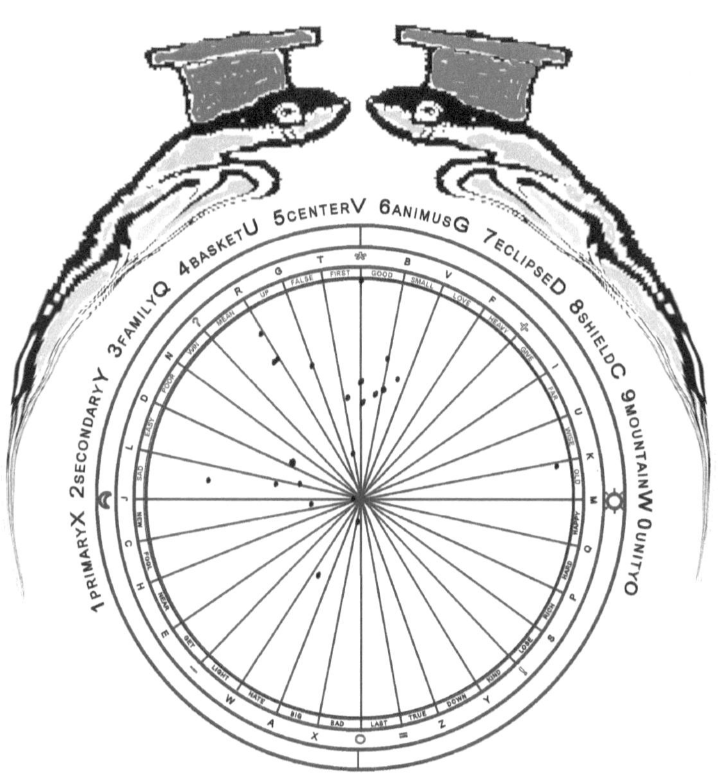

"You have entered a negative spiritual cycle. It is causing a lasting split in the mental plane interfering with common communication and it is irritating but you are not letting it get to you. Your mouth is unable to tell the truth about something from the past. You know what to do. You must utter the truth about the past event or thought and start the unwinding of the negative cycle."

Existence is possible if there is an area of concentration or diffusion in the otherwise homogenous.

What are you willing to lose to find yourself?

74

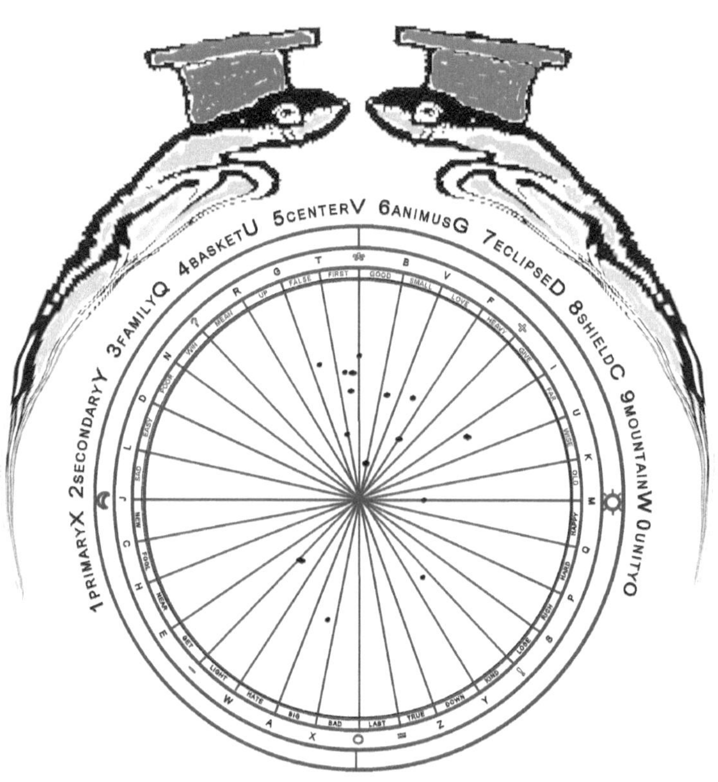

"Spiritually you are in silence. It is a restful silence supported by your mental attributes- emotion and intellect. This support is in the shape of a counter attack versus a negative psychic energy wave that you have mentally prepared to overcome. Small healing steps after the victory convert to powerful protecting love and the negative wave is banished beyond further influence."

Thousands of millennia after the Great Dissolution began, the Universe looked very different. Gravity was no more and all matter was decomposed and its energy dissipated across the endless black. The eight remaining Universal spirits silently reigned over the infinite darkness.

You are happy. You are light. You are full of love. You have something precious.

75

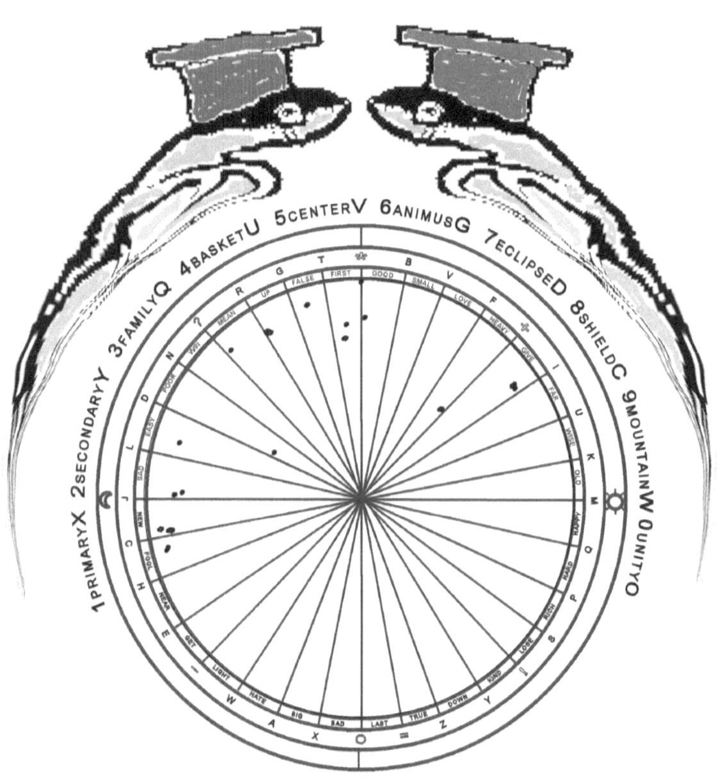

"The physical plane is overwhelmingly dominant. Your Spirit is quiet. Your Mind is considering its physicality. You are making yourself physically vulnerable through vocal activities. You have been injured but now must wait quietly until the proper time to deliver a physical deception. You must kindle your spiritual flames first by absorbing Male energy."

Nanet and her brother Nun ruled the endless waters. Keket and her brother Kek were masters of the enveloping darkness. Amanet and her brother Amun were lords of the encompassing clouds. Hehet and her brother Heh dominated the incredible expanses known as Infinity.

Alchemy always requires the application of energy, but it also requires the catalyst- Mercurius. The operator must convince him to act.

76

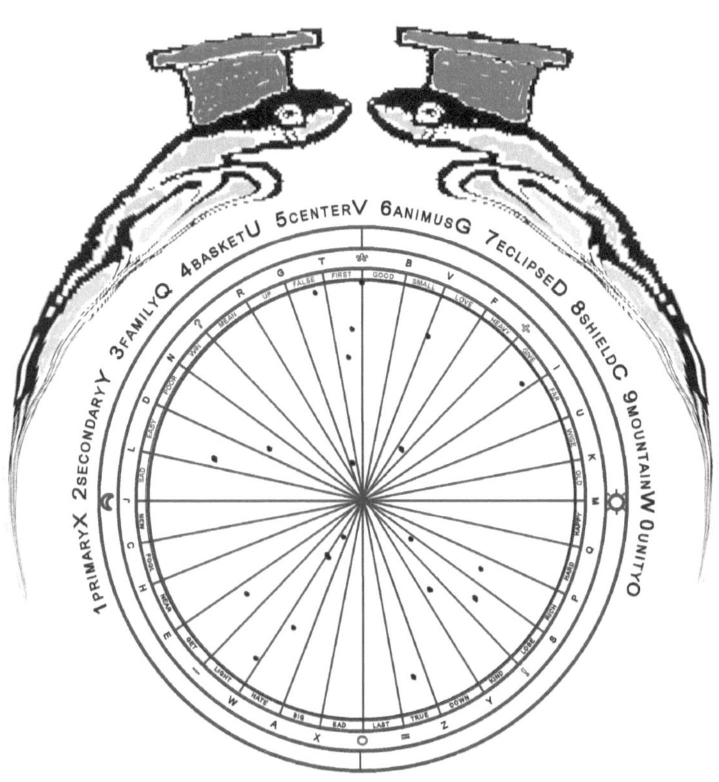

"The elemental and gender balance suggests this is a time for transformative change. Your Spirit has succeeded in casting off intense negative energy using your Male (scepter) sexual energy. Your Mind is focused and concentrated in a wave like pattern. Physically, your tremendous power is hidden. It is your Male sexual power- your magic scepter."

These eight beings honored as the Infinites wandered the empty planes abandoned by time. Feeling their way, they eventually found their counterparts amongst the shadows. Nanet was bound to Kek as the Flooding Darkness.

It takes power to rise every day like the sun.

77

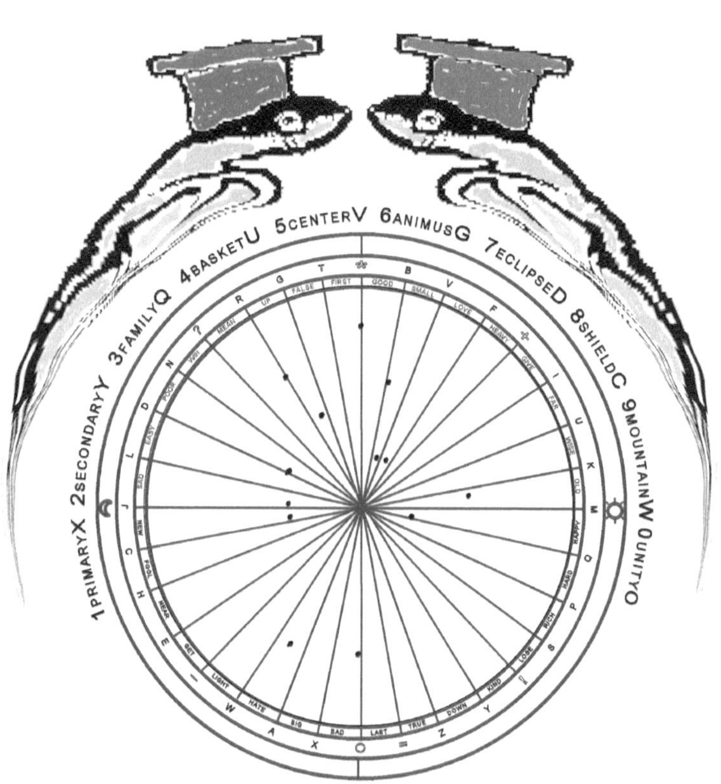

"You are in command of powerful forces enabled by a family bond. But you are undergoing a spiritual change that runs against the tribe. You keep silent but the new Spirit speaks for you putting you at risk. The new Spirit is your desire. There is a memory that is problematic for this spiritual change. Your physical Body is waiting for the outcome of the possible spiritual change or return to the past condition."

Keket shared the eternal night with Nun as the Burning Waters. Amanet shared her dominion with Heh as the Buried Infinity. Hehet was joined with Amun as the Neverending Obscurity.

The great mystery of how the body and soul communicate disappears when you realize your body IS you. It sends out your soul like a signal. It breathes your spirit.

78

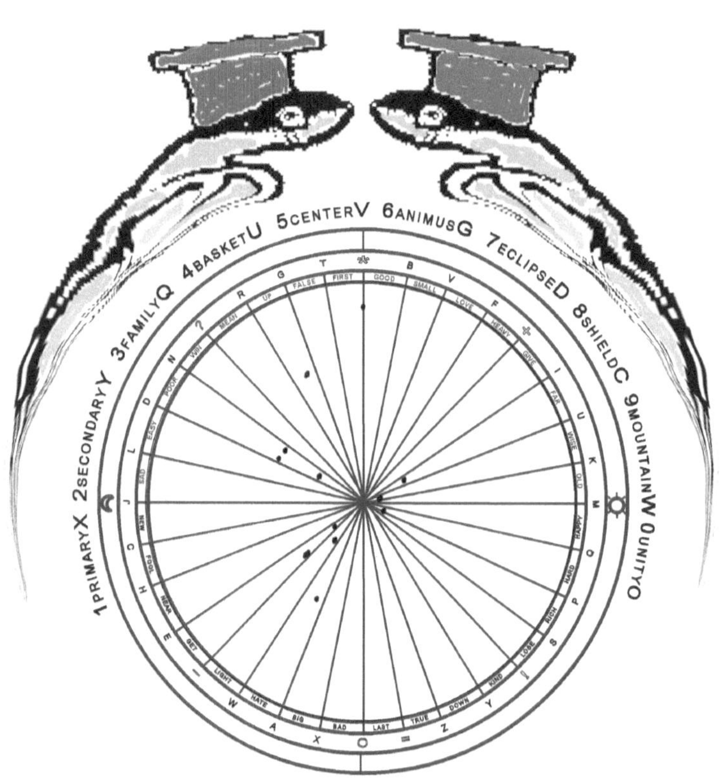

"The spiritual plane is dominant. Force is manifested as inspiration. You have come into possession of a useful magical concept in a spritual way, that is, non-intellectually. The Mind is held back to allow the Spirit to develop this gift from beyond. There is mental resistance to the restraint which is experienced as growing darkness."

Cold and silent they wandered until each pair, seeking solace in each other, simultaneously embraced in the abyss of night. With this act the eight were fused in a flash of forgotten light into Khepr the uncreated one, the New Rising Sun.

Existence is "written" as light on the dark background.

79

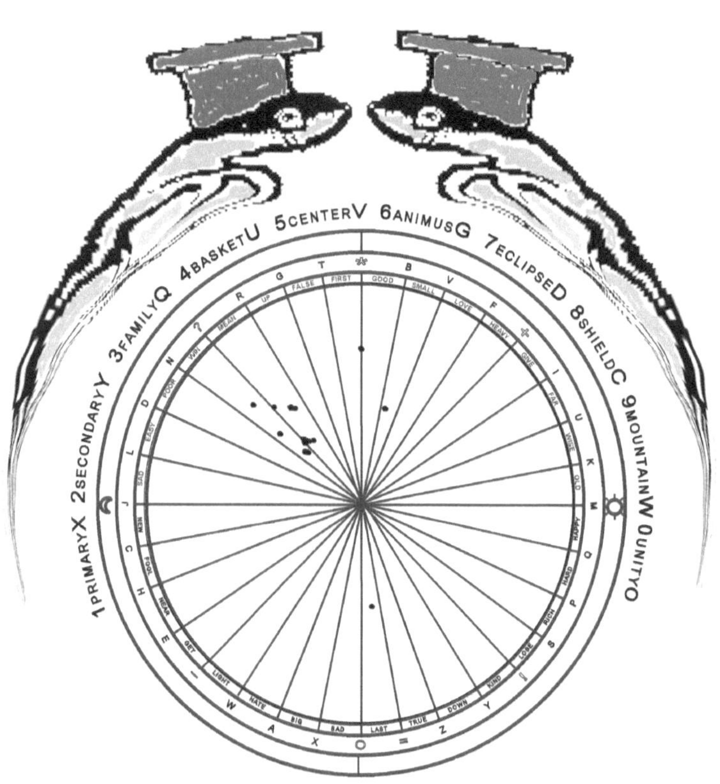

"This is only concerned with a single mental event. It is a relation of double mystery involving separation of two individual components. The component of importance is the larger of the two nearly equal parts. The mental process needs to be performed two, three or six times."

Ra- static power

Eye of Ra- dynamic power

Two aspects. Same being. The sun differentiated from the heat of the sun.

Cut the paws off the lion and let the green dragon soar. Kiss the moon's cheeks and descend once more.

80

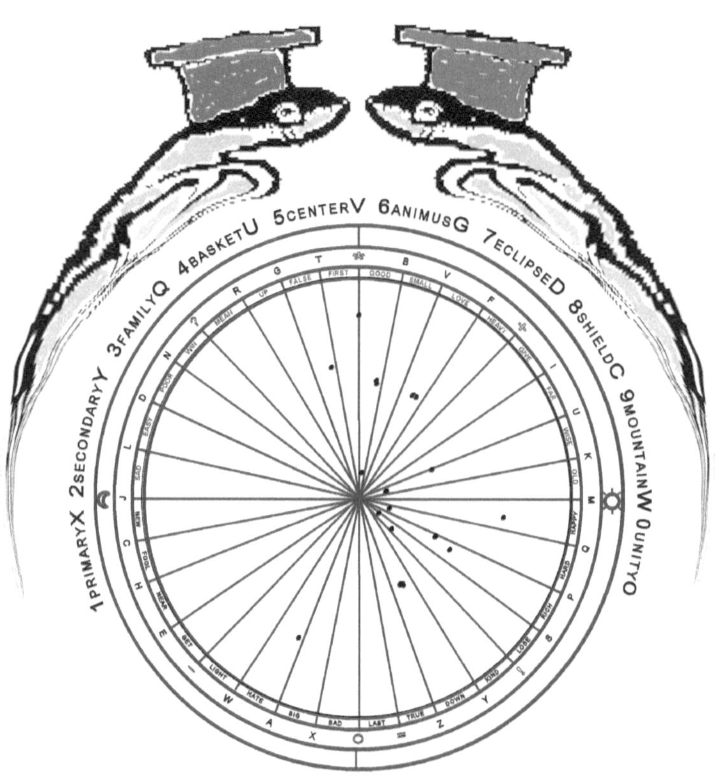

"There is a deep motion of the Spirit through the mental plane and toward the physical. The joy of the Spirit is charging the Mind causing a flood of new activity that will end in physical pleasure and happiness. The physical manifestation hasn't happened yet. There will be a rejection of an error as a component of this. Look towards the Body."

Your body is the gate between the planes.

What is truly hidden is yourself.

81

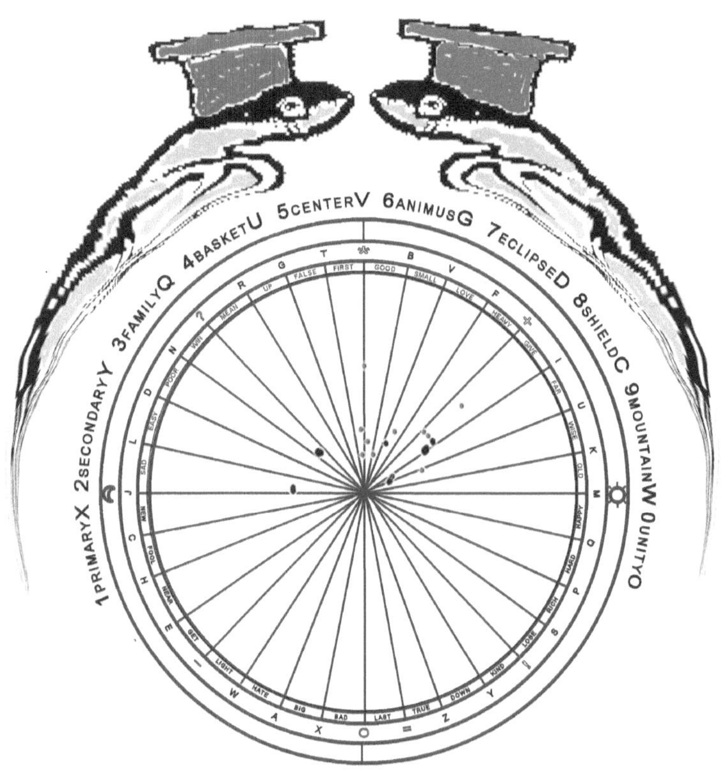

"There will be a symbolic "birth". Intuition yields strong emotional power manifesting in strong feelings of love for spiritual self and the world. This feeling gives incredibly powerful balance to the personality. It is the inward embracing the outward. The birth sign is revealed as an ego spirit or a name."

If you say it from your heart it must be true.

The Goddesses, The Eyes of Ra, are within you. You rule together.

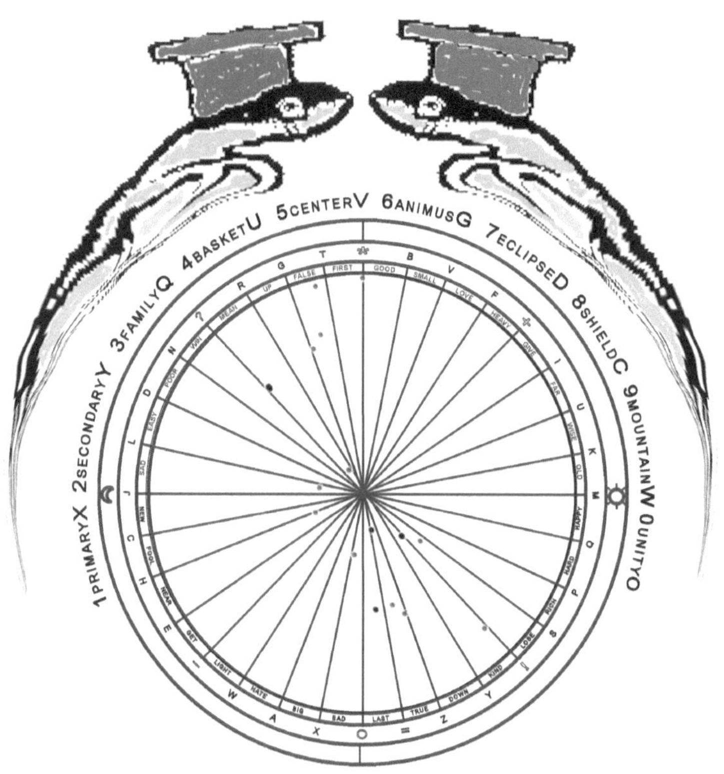

82

"You are taking leave of the spiritual plane and it worries you. Your intellect is working on a solution or even if one is necessary. It is experienced as a loss of truth. There is a powerful surge toward the realm of Body where truth is secondary to satisfying the means of organic life. There is physical danger that involves deception and false confidence."

The soul is made of flesh and blood.

Praise the awesome power and beauty of Hathor and the Eyes of Ra!

Give power to this rod! Let nothing resist my power and will as I hold this, my sacred rod! Let all others who dare touch it without permission serve me until they are released! Let the wisdom of the immortal voices in Duat be heard by the power of this rod!

83

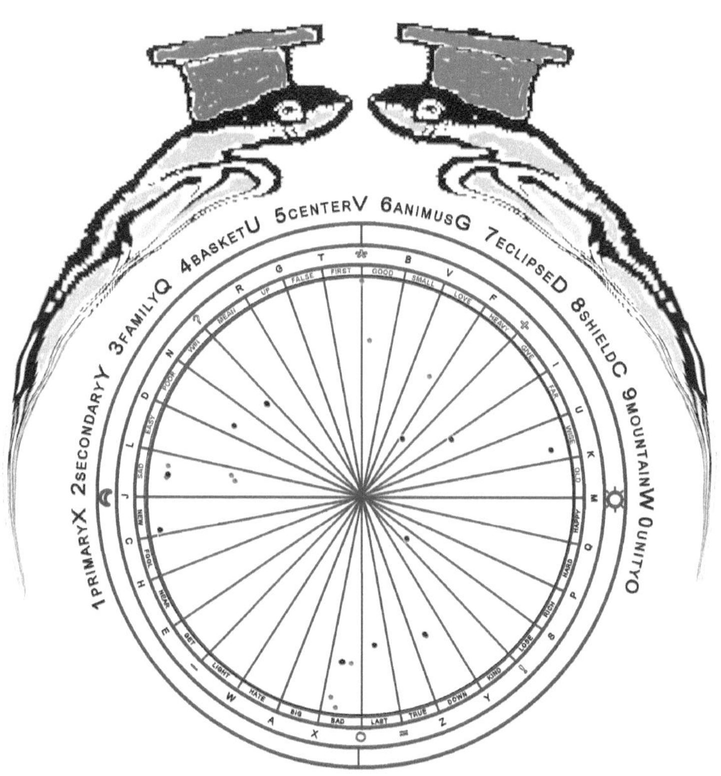

"You are undergoing a spiritual attack that is paralyzing. Negative mental energy is holding you prisoner but love remains to rescue you-albeit negatively. The solution offered is a shock to the Body in the form of an episode of intense lost love followed by a regenerating spiritual enlightenment."

Love and violence are twins.

Praise the Eyes of Ra! Praise Hathor the goddess of desire! I, Min, your devoted one adores you! Let us become one in pleasure!

Great Hathor, Eye of Ra, Goddess of Splendor and Music of Souls, Heartbeat of the World, Sensuous Serpent, Ray of the Mighty Sun Disc!

84

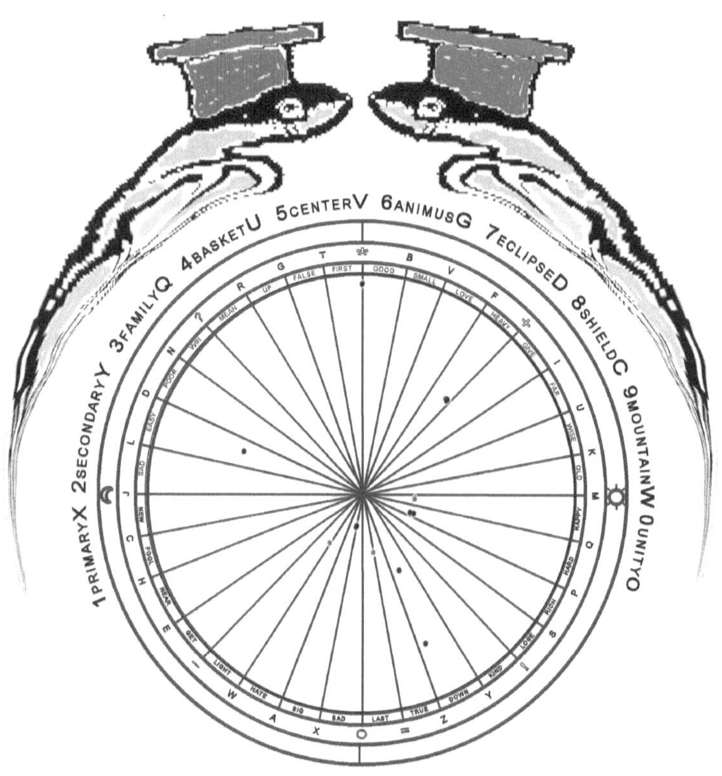

"The Spirit is penetrating into the mental plane to perform a specific task. There is a clear psychic journey from the Spirit to the physical. That task paradoxically is rooted in the Earth. The power of logic is brought to bear to increase stability and discipline and provide a psychic cleansing of the Body and bodily powers."

The number four is purely reflective. It is recognition.

Min- your ear, your stone, your chisel and horn- calls to you across the sands of Eternity. Share your wisdom, fire and charms! I cast my hook into the cascading waters of Isfit for you!

85

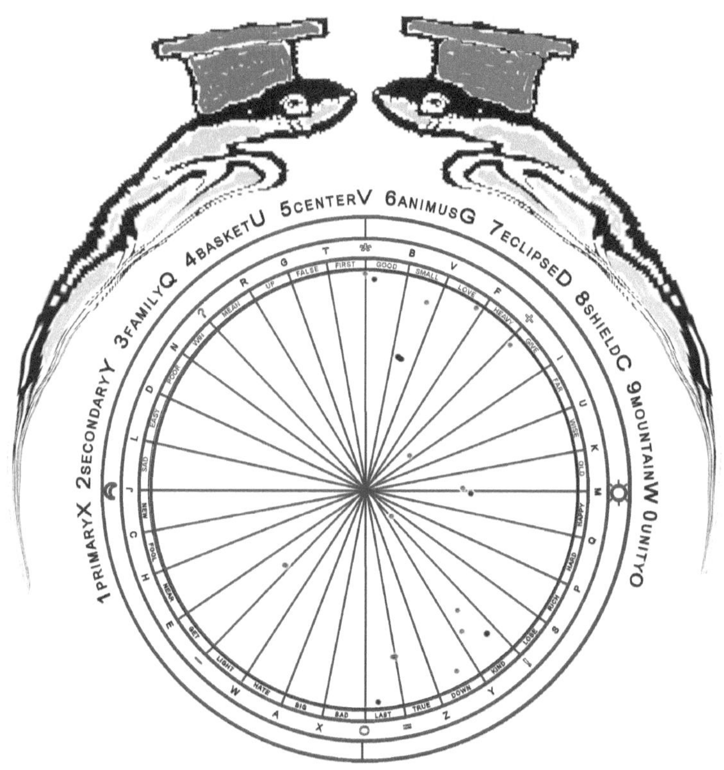

"You will receive two signs- one for each Crown, or gender energy. The mental physical link is fluid and strong, passing waves of energy back and forth. The signs will manifest as small, pleasure giving, permanent changes to the mid to lower Body signifying both Male and Female. Bodily love is heightened with the gender energy union. You have strong sexual attraction and convincing magnetism."

The Dyad is love.

Adornments of two kinds of metal enhance equilibrium.

86

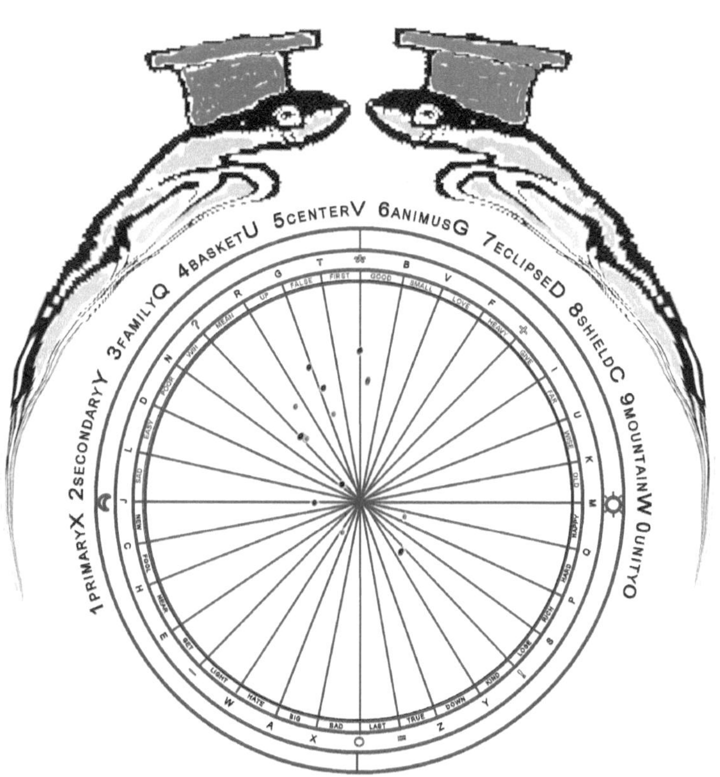

"You are undergoing an ascension of the Spirit requiring a sacrifice. Sacrifice may be self-sacrifice as well. Your intellect is leaving the event to your Spirit as pure intuition. It is a positive change that will toughen your thinking and appearance as you mentally apply it, but it actually fortifies your compassion."

You cannot change but you can be changed.

May our fear be a salve to our anger. May anger be our steel against fear. May knowledge conquer our foes. May love win the day.

87

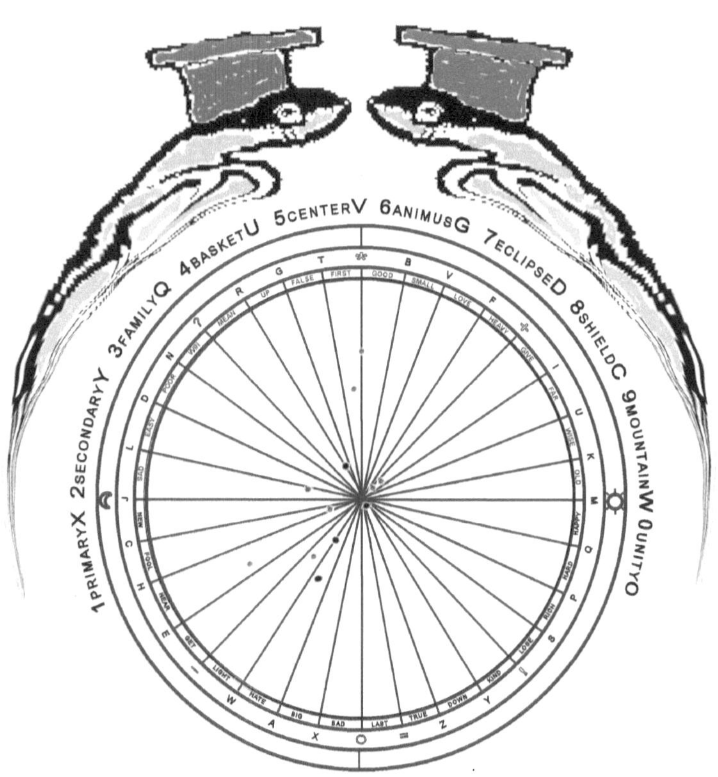

"You must cast a spell or make an evocation in the down/lower direction with an offering. You call on the Masculine energy and Fire element to assist you. This is the first step to acclimate the Mind to the dark processes that are within reach. Your balanced personality enables the grasp of these dark processes."

The Philosopher's Stone is a tension or oscillation between two opposite poles, one being the result of the reflection caused by the yielding impressibility of matter and its opposite, the reflection caused by unyielding resistance of a supreme spiritual force.

Do you have a soul- Yes. Do you have a spirit- Yes. Do you have an intellect- Yes. They are functions of your body- like your voice.

88

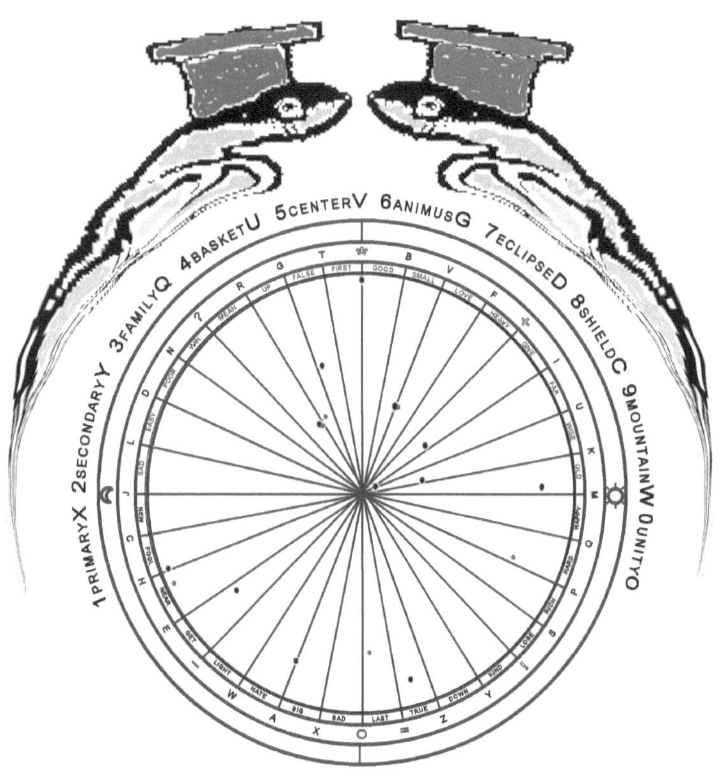

"The balanced energies let the physical reality of your sexual powers shine through. You agree to identify yourself as a sexual being after internal deliberation. Sexual stimulation is finally your path to truth and bridge to your ancestors."

Your body is a miracle. It created your soul.

There are two main spheres corresponding to the "two genders" which symbolize the static and the dynamic. One sphere is divination and the other is direction.

89

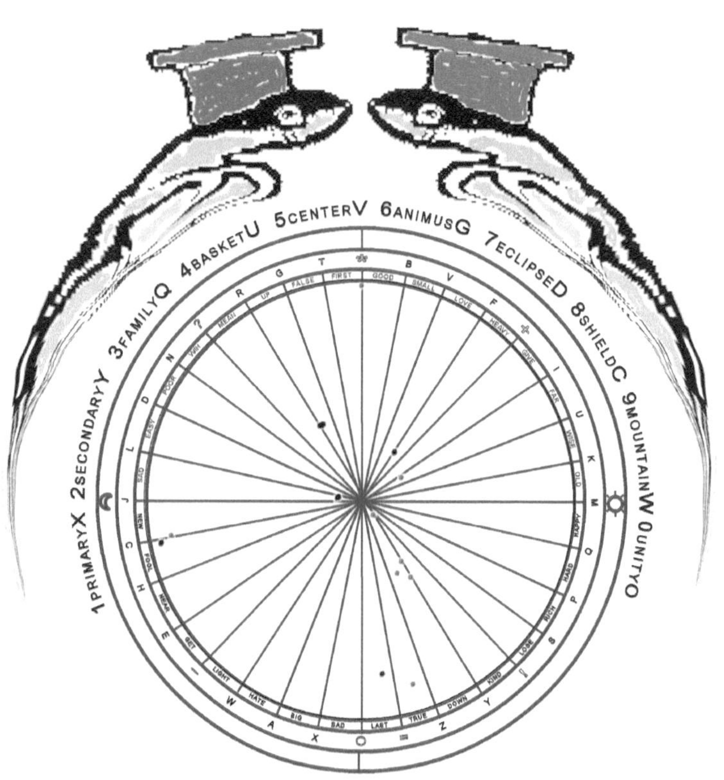

"You are concerned about a new object of devotion. A mental Fire is directed at the new spiritual presence and a dialogue results. The dialogue is about the saving and protection of the physical Body and can be trusted."

Honor the evolutionary goddesses the Eyes of Ra. They only exist through you. Through us. Their song is universal action.

Soul is the expression of a material structure.

90

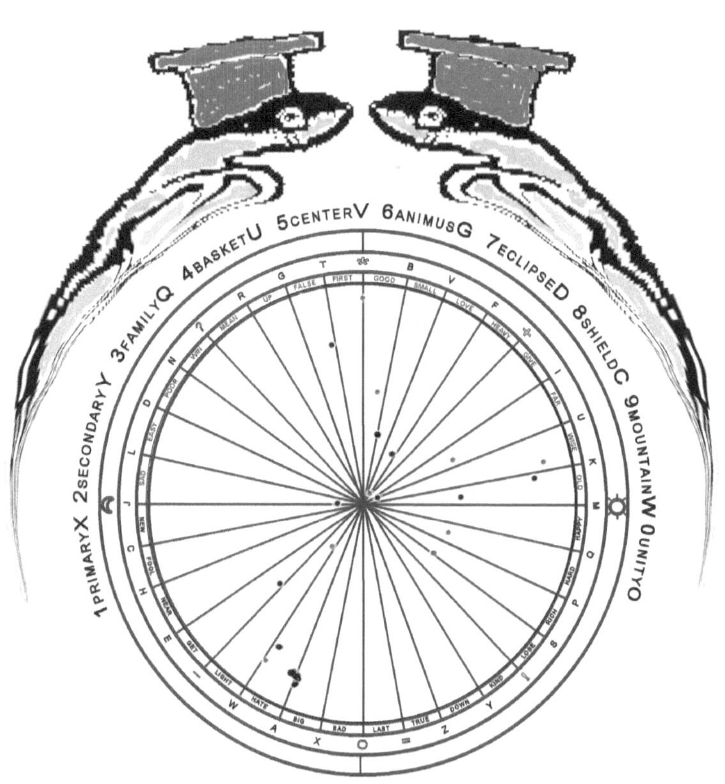

"Your devotion is toward a child and is strong and right. You are silently ascending on a difficult, ages old mental journey that will end in a negation that will be good for you but hard to understand. Both gender energies use the Male sexual power (scepter) in the prescribed and proper way."

Invoke Min, god of the black earth, before address-
ing the Eyes of Ra- if you sense they want it that
way.

Power is the ability to change.

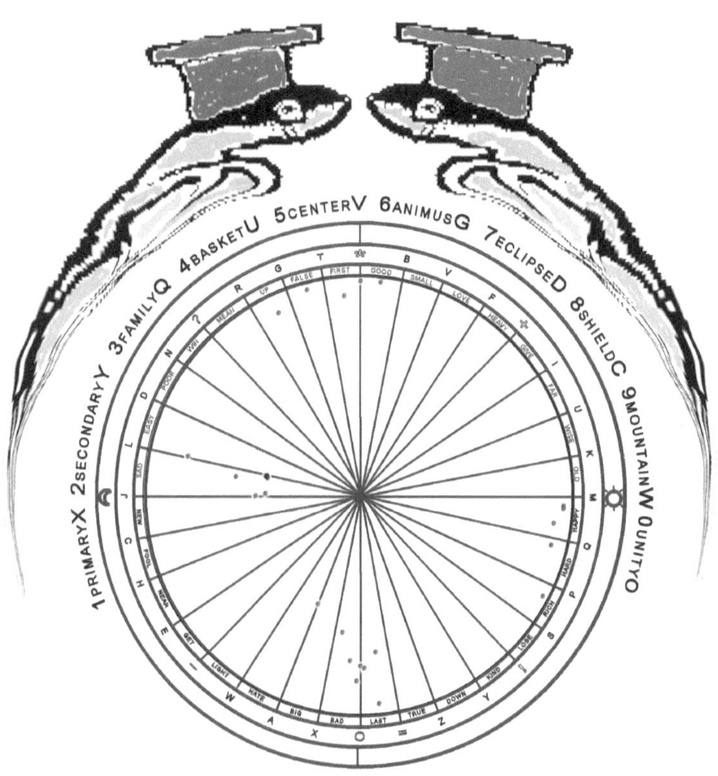

91

"The Spirit is disengaged. The Mind is frustrated. It is working on what is an insoluble problem concerning the ego (scepter) and its placement in the universal as aspects of the Spirit. The Body supplies a solution. Early on, the ego draws the Spirit to itself, and later the universal calls the Spirit out like the Body in morning (aroused) and evening (with sleep). Moderation, as with the Body, is key to spiritual health."

The same feeling that tells you a note is in tune is the feeling that tells you something is true.

The elixir of life is all around us. Drink it in.

92

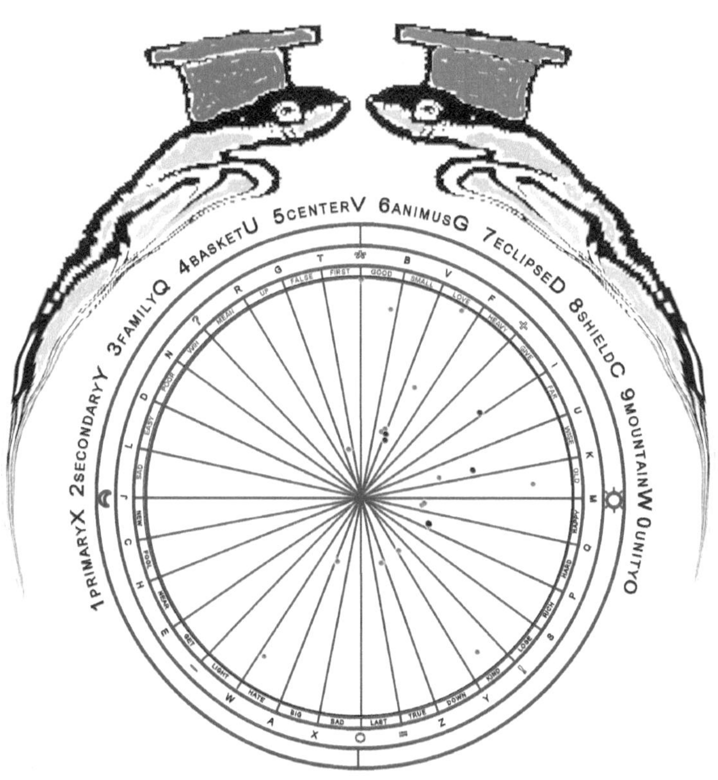

"The Mind is at work while the Spirit and Body take a secondary role. The Male sex drive is causing a boundary crossing that invites the Female into the workings of a warlike intellect. The Spirit is not really asleep but silent. The Mind is pleased by this clever use of the sex drive to increase power. The Sun and solar characteristics fuel this process, increase sexual performance, deepen sexual enjoyment and provide overall good health."

Khepr is the Sun Sphere and its Motion in one. A single but dual being. It finds itself in the midst of the Heavenly Waters, inexorably moving, creating the boundaries of the horizon.

You have eight faces.

93

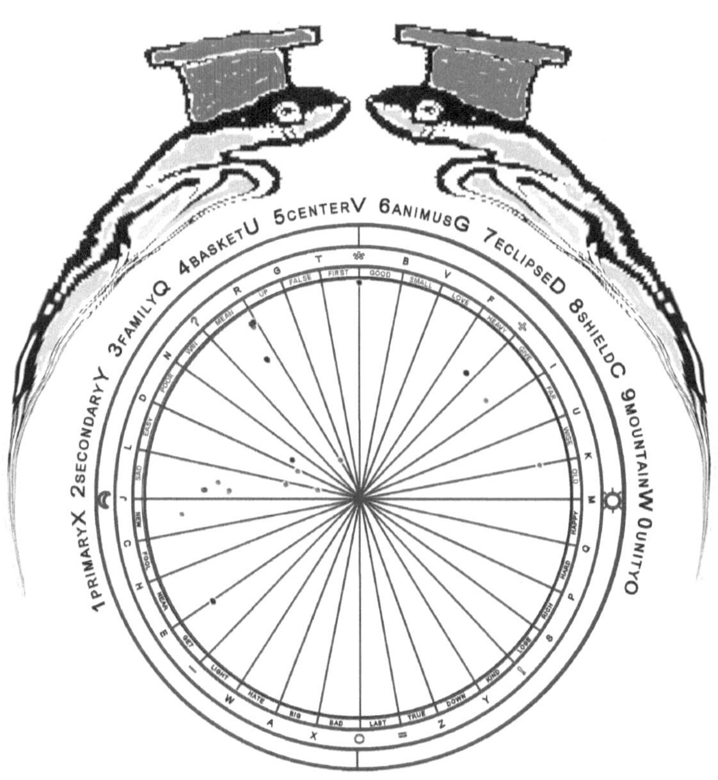

"Language or communication is the basis of Spirit and Mind. In the Mind the communicative power is in severe decline. The mouth is the proof and regenerative persuasive power. The mouth must perform aggressively to make a change. The Spirit waits."

The Sphere is Ra the golden, and the Motion is the Eyes of Ra- a different fabulous Goddess for each degree of intensity in the ceaseless movement. These two aspects are the static and dynamic principles.

No one can have the same spiritualism because it is simply the contents of the psyche. Your faith is yours and yours alone.

94

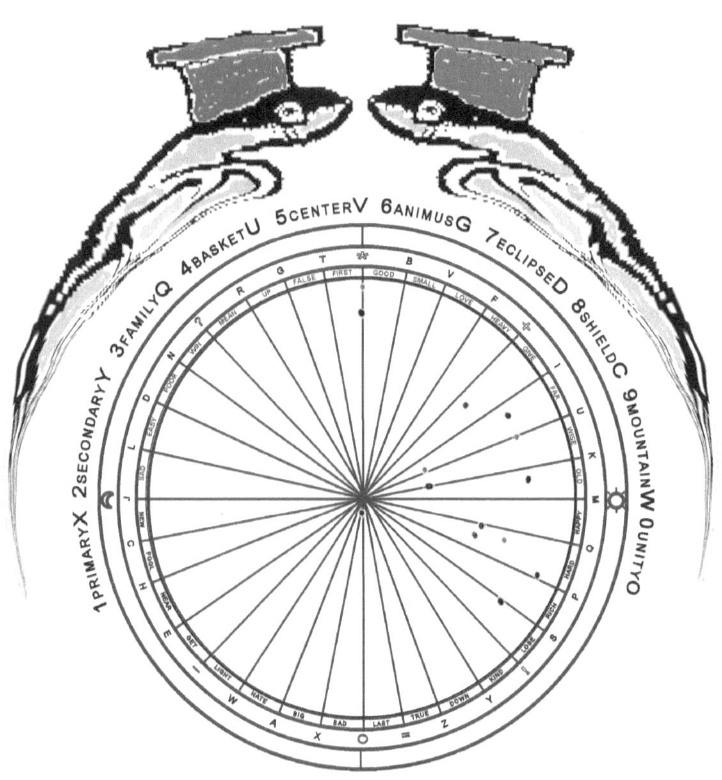

"The Spirit is strong, powerful and destructive. The Mind is sure of its bond with the divine Feminine which seems remote and difficult to reach. Physically there is both great age and great health shown by repeated signs of balance. This physical stability is vital to achieving union with the divine Feminine which will moderate and open the Spirit."

The Eyes of Ra create waves in the Heavenly Waters as they undulate. The waves in their turn ramify and become the four natural elements reborn into the universe.

When you realize how precarious life is, you become kind. When you forget and feel safe, then cruelty returns.

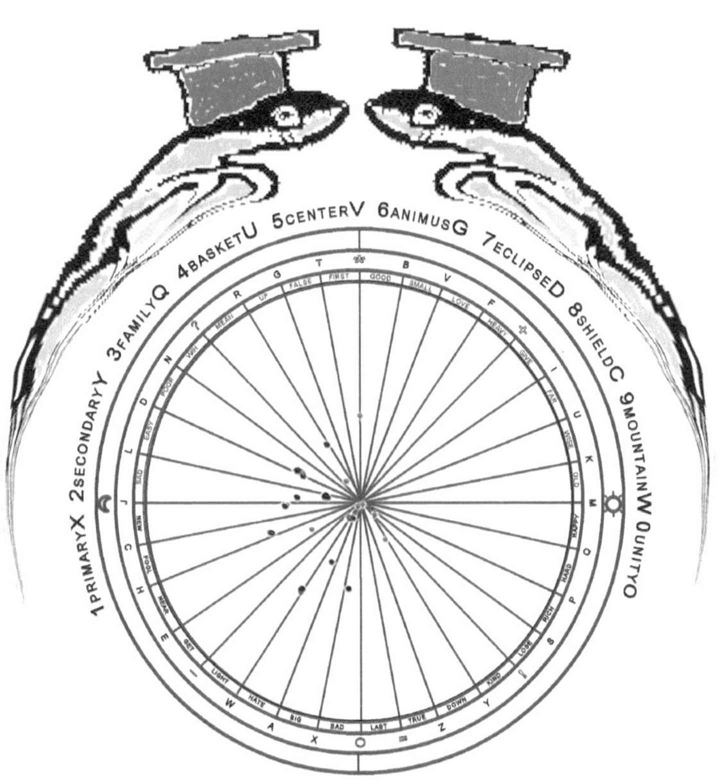

95

"This Spirit is highly dynamic and passes regularly between the normally dominant divine Female into the Male secondary energy to embrace the warlike Male aggressiveness at the cost of peace and intuition. This process is spiritual and mental, the physical is not present here. The Mind is actively thinking about the transition in an inner conversation. It determines that this split spirituality is a destiny for good or bad and the highest priority."

Set is the Fire of passion. Osiris is the Earth of acceptance. Isis is the Water of healing and Horus is the Air of intelligence. The mists finally clear and the Season of Ma'at begins as the cycle of Evolution is once again commenced to be repeated forever and ever.

The full Moon makes the heart beat faster.

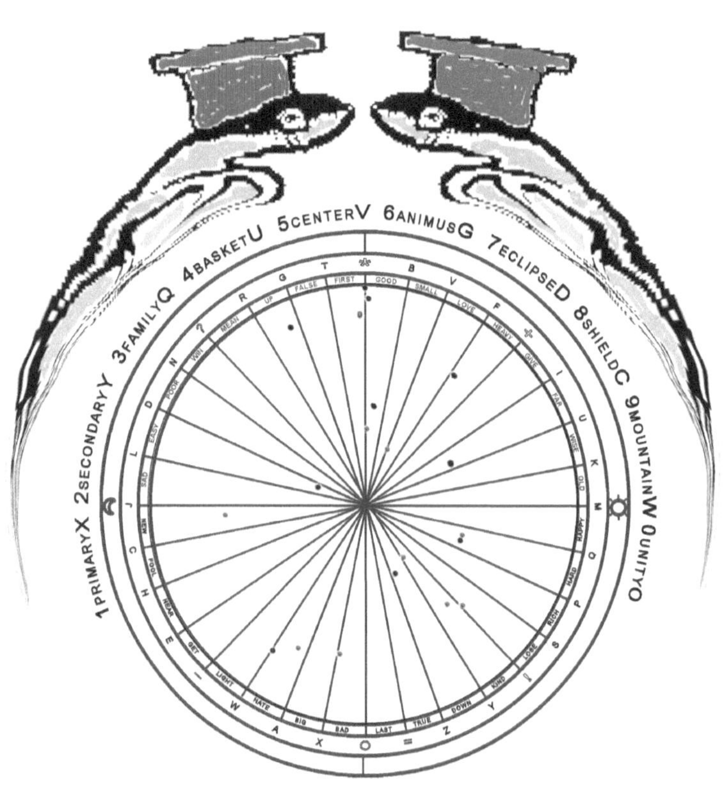

96

"It is a time of spiritual decline. The Mind is compensating. Safety and grounding are emphasized. The Body is under a related spiritual attack. The Body must maintain a raised position to ward off the attack. The Mind stabilizes through intense meditation on the physical. Positive growth will be ushered in by a new antagonism or opponent."

Man and the divine soon find each other and thrive. The famous priest builds a monumental temple. He is deified as Thoth, master of language and wisdom.

The Prima Materia isn't bad or flawed. It is all potential waiting to transform!

97

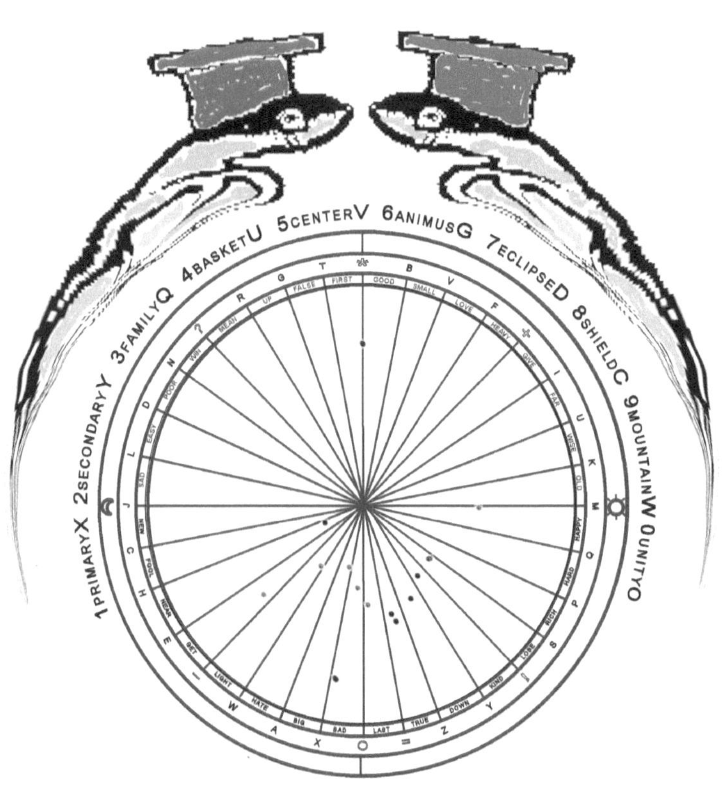

"The whole person is balanced in Spirit, Mind and Body. All facets are equally engaged. Both static and dynamic characteristics are manifested. Force and discipline are driving you now. You are not overthinking or overfeeling. It is a calm power. Your Mind is a powerful healer of the Body. Use that healing power."

He finds eight baby baboons in a corner of the temple and raises them as his own. A tradition carried on generation after generation. His descendants reign over mankind. Kings and queens tremble at his word.

Do not believe in free-will. The body decides, then the mind agrees.

98

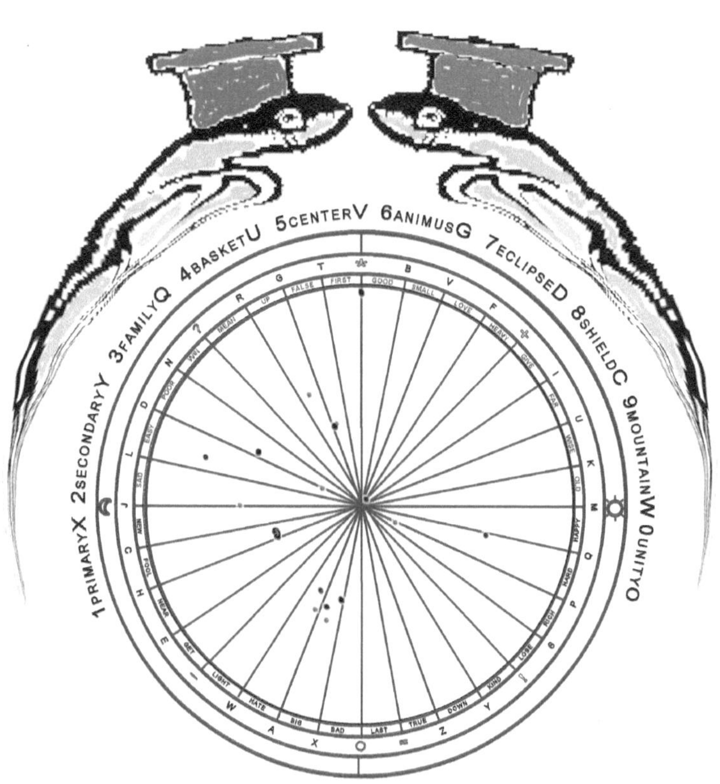

"The Spirit is in control of the Body. You are preparing a psychic Spirit attack that will devastate its target. The preparation involves a suppression of the mental and bodily activities during this time. The Mind is aware of the importance of this attack and is willing and helpful to Spirit. The Mind is singly focused on War and thoughts of family must be set aside to assure the efficacy of the psychic attack."

One day, in the temple, Thoth finds no fruit to feed the baboons, now fully grown. They tear him apart and devour him. They leave the temple together, four sets of siblings bound in pairs.

Alchemical transformation is great- but that additional power needs to be translated into action.

99

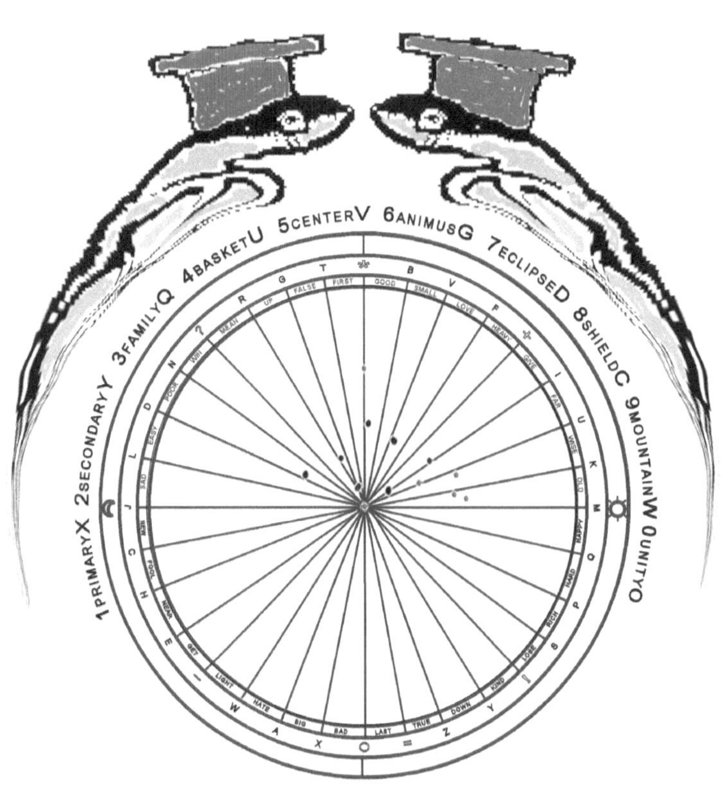

"Male energy loudly dominates the Spirit at the absolute center of the Self. But a Feminine energy guides the Mind from without in various intensities. This varying Feminine energy is the stabilizing and firm voice within. She is the ancient wise one that regulates the immense but impulsive spiritual power. This is done through both intelligence and intuition. It is a calm and ethereal balancing power."

Their power increases each day. They give each
other names and kingdoms. The temple is soon
buried and forgotten. Thus begins again the season
of Isfet, the Great Dissolution.

The evolving Goddess. Goddess of evolution.

100

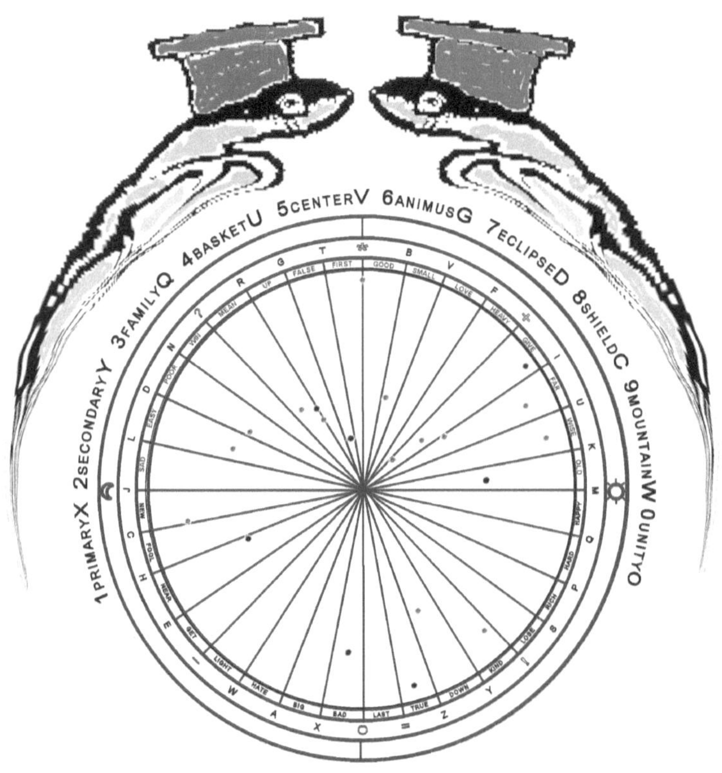

"The Spirit is transformed into its final shape. It appears Masculine but has Feminine elements within. The Mind is fully integrated with the Spirit through a special language that needs to be practiced in order to reach perfection. The physical Body is the protector of both Mind and Spirit. The head, chest and upper limbs strengthen the bond of correspondence. The lower limbs and generative areas weaken the bond. This allows for growth and truth."

The full moon is the red and the new moon is the green.

Even those who are skeptical of Astrology believe in Gravity. But they are related. Each heavenly body acts on every other heavenly body- even ourselves.

The Strange Transformations of an Electric Alchemist

December 24, 2025-

Sometimes life takes surprising turns. I never had any religious feelings or mystical inclinations. My opinion on these things was primarily that they were errors of thought. I had a passing interest in occult topics in relation to horror films, comic books and television shows, but like for most other people they certainly were not an occupation of any depth. Looking back through my early life, the only clue to my future alchemical pursuit I can think of was an interest in Egyptian Hieroglyphics that blossomed in an early grade of elementary school with a mild intensity and was then completely forgotten.

Fast forward to September 29, 2017. I'm married many years and working in the Safety Department of a large manufacturing plant. My wife and I are visiting her family in Europe. We've just arrived after a 10-hour flight, stay up as long as we can to counteract jetlag and then go to bed. I've made this journey many times and the quality of sleep when one's time cycle is out of adjustment can be bad. On this particular trip I was sliding in and out of very light sleep all night bordering on trance. The feeling was of deep meditation accompanied by a profound stillness of body. I heard a woman's voice. Clear with an unusual accent. She was telling me things and I listened intently for an unknown length of time. When I regained consciousness, I couldn't remember any of the content of the conversation. But I remembered the voice, and that's not all. I had an image in my memory- just some shapes. I had a notebook with me to write down original song lyrics, so I made a sketch of the image lingering in my mind.

Over the next several days there were more con-versations and more trances. The image took shape as a device of some sort. I could see the shapes of the components. I knew it was a device but I didn't know what it was for. I knew it had something to do with "crystal power" and my skeptical alarm was going off. I had never ever considered crystal power as anything but nonsense. The device was becoming more detailed each morning. By the time I returned home I knew what it would look like if I built it.

I made a decision. I could either forget about the whole incident and chalk it up as an audio halluci-nation, or I could go with the flow of the experience and follow it through to its destination. I clear-ly and soberly decided to see where the woman's voice would take me.

I started collecting materials online to serve as the components of the device. I had no sound informa-tion to work on- I just went with my gut. I wanted to make something that looked like the drawings. I was making detailed notes of the individual components and their costs. I found some parts in the trash on my job. It did not take too long and the device was complete. A crystal is at the heart of the device. I later did some research on crystals and their interaction with energy and found a basis for the "crystal power" of the device's operation.

I was home now sleeping normally, but sometimes I would rise out of sleep into a trance and she talked to me further. Again, the words are unknown to me. But there is another image. A spoked wheel. Later I discovered the similar round images of the psyche called "mandalas" explored in Jungian psychology. I knew I had to use the wheel as a kind of decoder. I intuitively made a list of word-pairs of opposites-polar pairs, to use in conjunction with the wheel. A particularly lucid trance fused the current images and ideas together. It was perfectly clear. I was to use the device and the wheel to communicate with the mysterious woman. I decided to refer to the whole setup as my "apparatus". The output product is an image based on the wheel which I named a *Violograph* after the word surfaced in a trance. I did a search online for the term and discovered that there was already an invention from the 19th century with that name, but I didn't think the inventor would mind if I used the term to describe the image. Then I set to work using the apparatus which is best described as a sort of divination lamp. I called the process of using the apparatus *Spectrolithography*.

At this juncture I gradually stopped hearing the woman's voice distinctly and her guidance came to me as intuition. She was becoming part of me. Our relationship became more integrated every time I turned on the apparatus and interpreted the resulting image. A detailed symbolic method to interpret the following messages was gradually unfolded to me in thoughts and dreams. The apparatus revealed to me her name and geographical origin. She is an individual person, but she is so old that she was also generalized into a Goddess because of her constant presence to many people over many millennia. She told me the name Hathor is an honorary title like *Queen.* I do not know how she came to inhabit psychic spaces. That was not revealed.

On November 05, 2018 I had an intuition that a scientific approach to art was expressed by Alchemy. In other words, I thought Alchemy was the practice of using scientific techniques to create art. I had been using the apparatus since March. I considered the Violograph image art. I knew nothing about the history or works related to Alchemy except that it was supposed to be an activity that led to the development of modern science. I didn't consider Alchemy again until I noted on April 27, 2020 that I experienced a "nascent wakening of consciousness". This intuition included the four classical elements and binary gender. It turns out these ideas are central to classical Alchemy. The first mention I have in my notes referring to the psychologist C.G. Jung is dated December 14, 2020. I had been researching Hermeticism, Neoplatonism and through them, Gnosticism, in an effort to understand the psychic changes I was undergoing. This led me to Jung, and I became acquainted with his basic ideas and extensive late career work on Alchemy. I was immediately struck by the correspondences between his analysis of alchemical concepts through history and my practice with the apparatus. Not only that, but his ideas about the development of the self by integrating the unconscious content of the psyche into the light of reason and consciousness lent a goal or destination to my seemingly endless transformations.

The correspondences that struck me are these. All the four classical elements, Earth, Air, Fire and Water have a function in the Spectrolithography process. Earth is represented by the crystal at the heart of the apparatus. Fire is the electrical energy converted to light. A water bath is needed to develop the output media. Air is used to apply the final fixation to the output media.

Gender is an essential element in Alchemy. The union of opposites symbolized by gender is what effects the actual transformation. Of course, some modern views of gender differ from classical views. Symbols reflect the culture they are used in. The thing to keep in mind is, that no matter the specific images evoked, Gender describes a system of dynamic movement between opposites in conjunction. Considered systematically, in my practice, the Female represents the dynamic moving power and the Male is revealed as the static unchanging force. These dynamic properties are embodied in the transformation "vessel" of Alchemy. My apparatus includes a version of the Vessel. The round copper vessel contains the oblong stone. The stone penetrates the vessel. The metal and the stone. The union of opposites. Yet they are intimately related. The transformation of the Alchemist's spirit can then also be considered as a kind of spiritual re-birth.

The Alchemist's forge is a common image in classical Alchemy. The fire that acts on the material is an essential component of the transformation process. The fire of my apparatus is electrical energy exciting the atomic gas of the central lamp. It is another correspondence that the metallic gas used in the lamp is Mercury.

Mercury, or Mercurius is the spirit of Alchemical transformation. This "spirit of matter" is contained in all things of the Earth. Sometimes symbolized as a bi-gendered being, Mercurius is the world soul trapped in the material realm. The goal of alchemical work is to release them from their material prison and compel them to effect the transformation.

Mercury is one of the three alchemical Substances. The other two, Salt and Sulphur, also have a place in my practice. Salt refers to the apparatus' crystal heart and Sulphur is my own psychic power. The three alchemical substances are related to the four classical elements in a union of opposites. The tension and identification between the numbers three and four are found throughout the literature of Alchemy as well as other occult sources.

Alchemical processes are always associated with color changes to the materials worked with. Spectrolithography is also defined by the color changes brought about in the output medium. The process starts in blackness and is then brought to the white.

The final reddening is the interpretation of the image and the delivery of the oracle. The colors address the stages of the transformation and their active agencies. The blackness of the black sun, or "niger sol" is the beginning of the change. It is the body and soul united in both the opposites of innocence and sin. It is a recognition of the need to transform and improve oneself. The black sun knows it will be re-born in the transformation and that it must die a symbolic death first.

The whitening is the transformation of the black sun, the united body and soul, into both a universal spirit and the individualized spiritual being. The two beings represented by the juxtaposed moon and sun images found everywhere in classical Alchemy. Mercurius is called upon to effect the whitening through the symbolic killing of the black sun and the separation of the body and soul. The body remains in the bottom of the vessel, and the soul is split into the two spirits that rise to the top. The universal spirit of Mercury as the Moon reintroduces the Alchemist to their other self as one of an infinite number of beings that are at the same time only one. The Sulphuric individualized spiritual "ego" being is able to fully sense its own solar power and existence.

The final color change, the reddening, is the last stage of transformation. It is the reuniting of the two spirits (as soul) with the body in a holy purified state. The spiritual renewal of the Alchemist is the goal of the alchemical work. The reddening is referred to by many symbols such as "making gold" or creating the Philosopher's Stone. The culminating reunification of the fortified, transformed soul with the living body is the thing that separates Alchemy from other spiritual practices. In my practice the reddening is the extraction of the Goddess's wisdom from the material realm and its reunion in me as human knowledge. Her wisdom then effects my total transformation.

To sum up correspondences, the material elements and substances, the forge, the colors, and the vessel appear either as actual components of the apparatus or as concepts involved with the Spectrolithographic processes.

The Goddess Hathor is central to my alchemical experience. She has multiple functions in the history of my personal re-birth. She is the Desire that prompts each heartbeat of life. She is a unique personality who lovingly guides me with her voice. She is the wise and beautiful Mercurial deity of transformation that is both matter and spirit, body and soul. She is my own opposite gendered anima-reflection and the deep universal unconscious of Jung's psychology that is finally and ecstatically united with my own ego and body revealing the true golden self.

Each use of the apparatus and each new transformation ends with a return to the body and the cycle is set to begin again. In her golden light and radiance, we will embrace anew. Praise Hathor and the Eyes of Ra!

T
G
FALSE
FIRST
R
UP
?
MEAN
N
WIN
POOR
D
EASY
L
SAD
J
NEW
C
FOOL
H
NEAR
E
GET
—
LIGHT
W
HATE
A
BIG
X
BAD

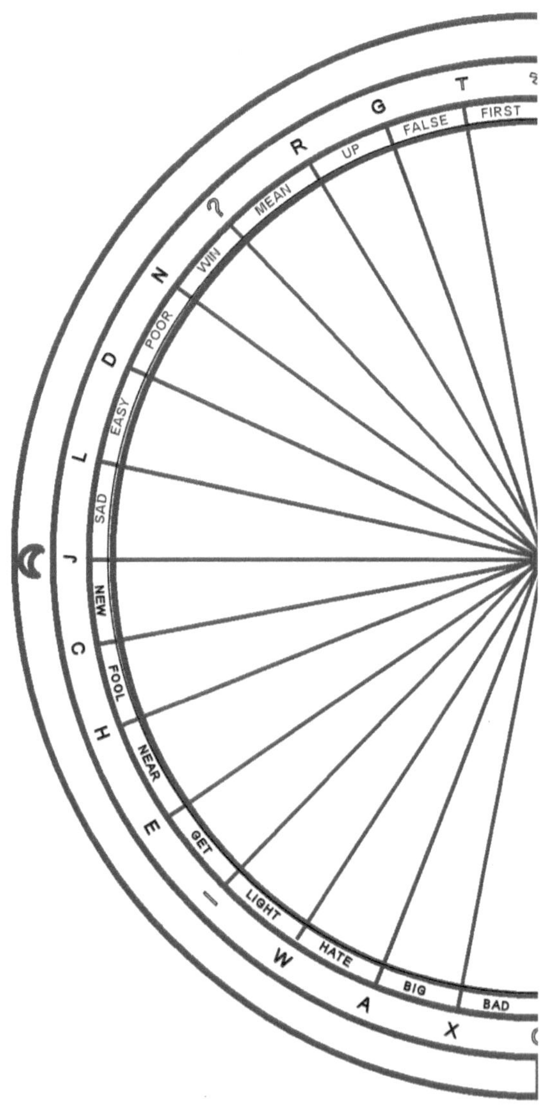

(Left)

GOOD
SMALL
LOVE
HEAVY
GIVE
FAR
WISE
OLD
HAPPY
HARD
RICH
LOSE
KIND
DOWN
TRUE
LAST
B
V
F
I
U
K
M
Q
P
S
Y
Z

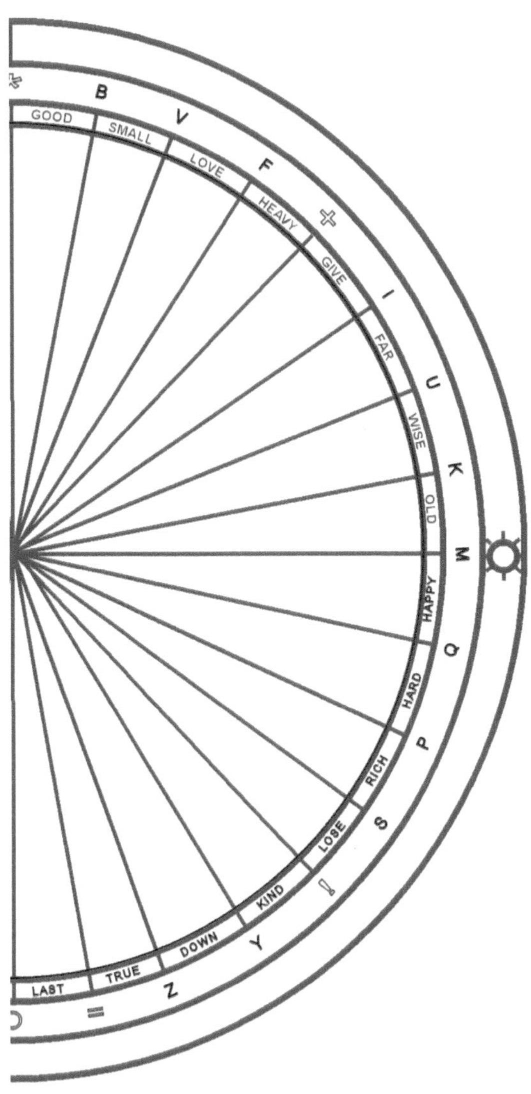

(Right)

<u>Dr. Howard C. Woodruff-</u>

The meditations accompanying oracles 53 through 65 were based on transcriptions from the notebooks of Dr. Howard C. Woodruff. He was my maternal grandfather and had a long career as an industrial chemist. He spent the last years of his life working on cures for cancer and HIV. When he passed away in 1997, I inherited his book collection which consisted mostly of moldering old chemistry texts. They had not been stored properly, and most were thrown out right away. But his laboratory notebooks were in good shape along with some of his short books and magazine articles. He was born in 1912 and spent time in Europe in the late 20's and early 30's learning chemistry at respected institutions. I remember him saying that he left there when the brown shirts showed up.

I didn't take the time to review these collected materials until my alchemical work was well underway. I was intrigued when I discovered his notebooks from Europe revealed an interest in Alchemy and early investigations into chemistry, particularly the work of Louis Pasteur. It turns out my grandfather invented an unusual electrical apparatus to heat chemical agents with sparks and recorded the results. He also described other inventions with obscure uses. Recently, I followed one of his formulas and recreated one of his experimental medicines. I'm hoping to compile his written works at some point in the future.

<u>Annie Nacht Morgan</u>-

Annie Nacht Morgan created the cover artwork and design for this book. I saw her work online when I was looking for an artist to help me with the project and I immediately knew she was *the one.*

Annie started taking classes in oil painting in 2021, during and after being sidelined by severe chronic nerve illnesses and multiple surgeries. Bedridden and in pain, unsure what was ahead for her, she persevered and learned how to paint at the same time she was learning how to cope with the challenges of a new physical reality.

Her skills developed steadily through commissions and the production of the *Painted Molecule Series,* which I found to resonate so completely with my Alchemical work.

She says that each piece she worked through taught her new lessons covering mediums, styles, brushes, and techniques, but that the process, difficult like "being pulled through a vise", left no room for error, or even a chance to discover more of herself in her work.

A 2025 visit to Frida Kahlo's home and studio, Casa Azul, in Mexico City had a profound impact on her personal journey. She realized she had to pour her SELF onto the canvas and into her working process. Like Frida, another woman who suffered deeply and yet transcended suffering, Annie returned home changed- and with a new artistic vision.

Annie reclaimed the "Nacht" from her maiden name, "Fosnacht"; Nacht, meaning "night" in German, reflected her recent painful history, her love of the night, and a new impulse to use layers and expressiveness, as evidenced in her *Study of Self Reclined On Table*. She is committed to exploring, through her art, the creation of works that deeply resonate with her authentic self and others.

The work she did for the cover of this book marks another evolution in Ms. Nacht's artistic vision. I'm proud to say that the cover design, which uses multiple layers of images, textures, colors, symbols, and documents, was one of her first forays into this medium. The rich layers form the digital collage, utilizing hand-painted textures, historic and found images, and symbols into a narrative book cover.

Praise the Eyes of Ra!

THNX VLI